W9-ADW-725

LAW AND GOSPEL

A Theology for Sinners (and Saints)

William McDavid

Ethan Richardson

David Zahl

Mockingbird Ministries

Charlottesville, VA

MOCKINGBIRD

"*Those who are well have no need of a physician, but those who are sick; I have come to call not the righteous but sinners.*"

–Jesus, in Mark 2:17

The authorship of this booklet is a collaboration between William McDavid, Ethan Richardson, and David Zahl, Mockingbird's three full-time staff members. Special thanks are due to Edward Bennett, Todd Brewer, Jacob Smith, and Aaron Zimmerman, for their feedback and insight as readers; C. J. Green and Evan Brush, our copy-editors; Paul Walker and Christ Church, Charlottesville, for their invaluable help over the years; Paul F. M. Zahl, as a father, friend, mentor, and theologian; and our readers, writers, and donors for their continued support.

Spring 2015

Contents

INTRODUCTION

Many have said that if it weren't for much of the Bible, church might actually seem like a good idea. It's hard to blame them. For all the great stories in the Hebrew Scriptures—of Noah and the Ark, Jonah and the Whale, Moses and the Red Sea, Joseph and the Technicolor Dreamcoat—there are countless more that paint God as not such a suitable father figure.

For example, in the book known as 1 Chronicles, King David is doing something wonderful: After years of his people forgetting God's rules, David is finally bringing back the Ark of the Covenant to its resting place in Jerusalem. Along the way, it is a very glorious scene, with David leading the way—harps and lyres and cymbals and trumpets are parading God's righteous rulebook through the desert and back to the Holy Land. It is an occasion of momentous celebration.

And then, in just two short verses, everything is shot to hell. One of the oxen pulling the Ark stumbles and, in an effort to keep the Ark from falling to the ground, a well-intentioned worshiper named Uzzah reaches out to keep it steady:

> "The anger of the Lord was kindled against Uzzah; he struck him down because he put out his hand to the ark; and he died there before God. David was angry because

11

the Lord had burst out against Uzzah; so that place is called Perez-uzzah [literally, 'Outbreak Against Uzzah'] to this day" (1 Chr 13:10-11).[1]

This blip of God's inscrutable wrath against poor Uzzah is just one of hundreds in the scriptures. For all the moments of God's deliverance and promise, there are as many moments when nations get burned, women and children get slaughtered, and faithful followers get put to shame. In these stories it's hard to find any inspiration. And worse, they often foul up the air of inspiration that the others bring.

These are definitely the stories that tend to speak loudest in the cultural picture of Christianity. Wrath has become synonymous with Christianity: unforgiving moral stringency, rampant judgmentalism, and self-indulgent certitude. And it is hard not to believe that these components have had a hand in the declining number of 'believers' in America and Europe. The church has stirred up a league of burnouts.

But even more than religious browbeaters, a God of judgment contradicts something huge in the larger culture, and that is our optimism. Today, more than ever, we believe in our own inherent giddy-up. A recent poll showed that around 96% of people within the millennial generation are sure that they will "get where they want to be in life." In 1950, a similar poll showed that only 12% of the same age group agreed. More than churchy judgmentalism, the God of Christianity—and his obstinate stance on human sin and helplessness—is an offense to the zeitgeist of humanist progress and potential.

For better or worse, our optimism is more than just the jolly updates we read on our social media feeds or the saccharine 'reality' love stories we see on primetime television. Our optimism could be described as a faith system of its own. Despite much

---

1. Unless otherwise noted, all Bible quotes are from the New Revised Standard Version (NRSV).

evidence to the contrary in the world around us, it involves the adamant belief that our lives are within the bounds of our own free choice and good judgment. Like the millennials in the statistic above, we tend to look expectantly ahead into some future assumption of progress, believing we will arrive there by our own gradual steps of self-betterment. And those steps of self-betterment are always achievable, always attainable, so long as one remains firm in one's optimism.

With any belief system, though, the rubber meets the road in daily experience—which is where optimism has a lousy track record. While self-help and science-of-happiness books fill whole quadrants of bookstores, the fact that business is booming is a verdict unto itself: We may buy each new bestseller on the power of positivity, but each fresh purchase suggests its lack. As much as we wish it were true, we can't seem to prove that the positive thinking industry is working itself out of a job.

On top of this, the sheer cruelty of life is far too murky for anyone to actually navigate. No amount of self-propulsion keeps us safe from what we are powerless against—that our twins are in the NICU, that our company is making cuts, that our investments have gone sour. And these are just the 'simple twists of fate.' It doesn't even account for the daily tastes of powerlessness we so subtly know as we go to bed each night: our recidivistic thoughts, our insatiable narcissism, and finally, our inevitable deaths.

It doesn't take a rocket scientist to see that optimism takes us no further than where we started, with poor Uzzah, slain despite his best efforts to uphold God's rules. His story, just like ours, is really about the myth of *control*, the kind of control that this righteous and implacable God declares we do not possess. And this is also why the world of optimism is not so different from the world of God's wrath. While we may operate every day under the illusions of control, even our best efforts at maintaining it ultimately fall short. As the Good Book says, "the wages of sin is death."

He doesn't sit well with us, this God of ours. And it's not like the New Testament makes any comforting amendments to God's 'Rules for Living.' In fact, when Jesus arrives on the scene as the Son of God, he ups the ante. He tells his followers that the Ten Commandments which sat in that Ark were not just about the actions of the body, but the intentions of the heart as well. He takes our optimistic self-appraisals and makes Uzzahs out of us all.

What, then, can be done? What does a church (with impossible standards) have to say to a culture burned by optimism?

Martin Luther understood that God has spoken and continues to speak in two words: Law and Gospel. Law is God's moral measure, the command for good and right living, the just requirement to be perfect. The Law is good, but the Law is also our condemnation. While Christianity upholds the Law of God, it also makes the undignified claim that this Law proves us to be a stubborn and obstinate people, fundamentally turned away from the right choices, the proper feelings, the good life. The Law, for Martin Luther, brings humankind face-to-face with its death sentence.

The second word, Gospel, means 'good news.' While the Christian faith argues that the problem within us is worse than we'd ever admit, it also proclaims that God has moved into that problem with love and sacrifice. The 'good news' is Jesus Christ, who died and rose from death, taking the whole of God's wrath upon himself and setting us free. In short, while we are all Uzzah, we escape Uzzah's punitive fate by the all-encompassing love of God, which speaks louder than his voice of wrath.

These two words are what this short book is about. For those who for years have seen the Bible as all gloom and doom, understanding this distinction between Law and Gospel allows us to see the Bible in a new and enlivening way. It is also a trustworthy lens for understanding the Christian faith. More importantly, though, in a world done in by positive thinking, it is a means for *real* hope, a way to connect that understanding to life as we live it every day.

THE LAW

The Law as Imperative

In January of 2010, a boy whom we'll call Tom was preparing to take the SAT, the most common test for scholastic aptitude for college applications. Tom had always underperformed in school, the way his Ivy-League educated parents saw it. Given their brilliance and consistently high achievement, they thought there was no way that Tom was anything other than elite college material, blaming the school's teaching methods and claiming that a couple of the teachers just didn't like their son. They saw college as an opportunity to finally let their son's true potential shine, but his GPA was on the low side. They hired a top-notch SAT tutor, and Tom, convinced by his parents' belief in him and excited to finally excel, dedicated several hours a day to test prep. When he scored a 1500, everyone was thrilled: his credentials finally reflected his presumed ability. With the help of his high score and some connections his parents still had, Tom got into two Ivy Leagues and chose Princeton.

What happened next didn't surprise the college counselor (or the couple's competitive friends), but it stunned the family. Tom got to Princeton and floundered terribly. He had to work twice as hard as his classmates to keep up, and his classmates were studying for hours every day. He barely stayed afloat and passed for his first two and a half years, and then he had a mild breakdown and voluntarily dropped out. Disillusioned, he spent the spring and summer of his third year at home, and then was able to transfer to a state school near his hometown. He's recovering now, and has come to terms with the facts that he's not Ivy League caliber and that he likely won't be able to go to medical school, work in New York finance, or get into a top law school. But he's looking to begin a more normal career in a big city about two hours from home, and he's glad he learned his true ability sooner rather than later. His parents still don't quite understand why he dropped out, but they're starting to come around.

There's a good reason why so many churches have the Ten Commandments hanging on their walls. In Christian terms, we talk about God's demand for us to "be perfect... as your heavenly Father is perfect" (Mt 5:48) as God's Law, the moral requirements for how we should live our lives. This Law is the center of ethics for Christians, and people tend to feel guilty when they break it. But in addition to this 'capital-L' Law, there are also demands we feel every day from our culture, those around us, or ourselves. These expectations could be called 'little-l' law: to be an Ivy League student isn't mandated in any religious tradition or system of ethics, but Tom certainly felt the same complex of pressure, guilt, and disillusionment that he would have over an actual moral failing.

In this theology of Law and Gospel, a basic tenet is that *we can better understand our relationship to the Law of God by examining our relationship with little-l law*, because the psychological impact of them is often the same. The little-l law—'Thou shalt be beautiful' or 'Thou shalt be successful'—is often more measurable than the Law of God, as well as more salient in people's lives. That is, the pressure to be well-liked or valued at work is often stronger than the pressure to be a perfect person, and while holiness is usually invisible, things like salary, number of social media followers, and body weight can be easily measured. So it's easiest to talk about law where most people, regardless of beliefs, actually live: to start from the bottom up.[2]

The Law is first a command, an order for us to live in such a way that God is honored and human flourishing is maximized. It gives us a picture of the good life—imagine a community which obeys all the commands of God, one that successfully avoids anger, pride, envy, lust, and greed. God commands his people to do these things so that "all may go well with you and your children after you" (Dt 12:25). What more could you ask for? We know exactly what we must do to live good, full lives, and to give our children their best chance at doing the same. The Law is like a loving father making his child go to bed early, later making her do her homework, and later forbidding her from drinking and driving.

So the Law is, in itself, "holy and just and good" (Rm 7:12), as St. Paul writes. Secular demands, or 'little-l' laws, are also frequently just and good. Intelligence is a gift, something desirable, so it makes sense for Tom's parents to hope for that in their child. A top-notch education is better than a middling one; Tom's parents realize this, too. But it's a tough world, and very likely Tom had internalized their expectations to the point that he did not need more pressure than he was already placing upon himself.[3] But little-l laws may also be distorted versions of God's Law, areas in which measurable achievement and progress promise

---

2. This idea of theology from the bottom-up is only the first instance of a huge debt this book owes to Paul F. M. Zahl's *Grace in Practice: A Theology of Everyday Life* (Eerdmans, 2007).

3. Not only can conscience be socialized, but also some form of it exists inherently—the Law's requirements are inscribed in the human heart (Rm 2:15).

to allay the basic senses of inadequacy, guilt, and status-anxiety in fallen humans. Small arenas in which we can be big fish, can resume the quest of being "like God" (Gen 3:5). The deep desire to be more than human drives us to find *somewhere*, whether body or profession or society or political views—where we may attain that ever-elusive righteousness.

Furthermore, the Law of God and our little-l laws—which *coincide in the ways we experience them*—do not seem to produce what they command. They often backfire, and examples of this abound: Overweight people may lose weight under pressure from friends and family in the short run, but usually gain it back (and then some). Criminals tend to benefit from support, while ceaseless censure produces recidivism, or re-offending. One of the most puzzling aspects of human behavior is our ability to know exactly what we should do—on everything from keeping up with laundry to abstaining from adultery—and fail to do it.

The Hebrew Scriptures, which begin with the Fall, explore this persistent moral failure. From Genesis on, one of Judaism's many great contributions to the world was a deep awareness of humans as inherently sinful and rebellious. The great heroes of other ancient cultures were strong and clever and virtuous, but the great Jewish heroes copulated with slaves (Abraham), showed they were willing to allow others to have sex with their wives (also Abraham), cheated their brothers, seduced their in-laws, murdered, started civil wars through terrible family decisions, yet somehow—through a mixture of humility, near-insanity, and good fortune—served as conduits of God's action in the world.[4] The nation of Israel's entire sacred history consists in its rejecting God's ways over and over again in preference to their own, yet finding that God's faithfulness vastly exceeds their obedience. This utter inability to do what we know to be good is at the core of the Hebrew Scriptures' view of human nature, and such pessi-

---

4. After Abraham, Jacob, Tamar, Moses, and David, respectively.

mism is only intensified in Christianity.

Contemporary American culture, however, holds a much more optimistic view of human moral capabilities than does the Bible, and this has unfortunately crept into churches. How else to explain the fact that a religion based on acknowledging our own faults and shortcomings has become widely associated with extraordinary judgmentalism and self-righteousness? American Christianity now is in crisis, in large part because people have marketed it as a religion of good people getting better, when in fact it is a religion of bad people coping with their failure to be good. In a culture which seems to assume our ability to advance, which strives to get enough information to make the right decision, the age-old message that even the best of us "do not do what [we] want to do" (Rm 7), tends to get ignored. The idea that we can always improve ourselves and attain our goals is not a harmless misconception, but instead lies near the root of much burnout, disillusionment, resentment, and religious recession.

Reading a book like this one will not help a bit with this destitution of willpower and tendency toward self-sabotage, but it may help explain a thing or two about why, from a Christian perspective, we're stuck in the place we are. Those problems, which could also be called sin, are best observed in our complex relationship to what we *should* do, or what we know is best for us, i.e., the Law of God and (sometimes) the expectations of society. We experience the Law as a measure of our worth, as a temptation to assert control, as an accusation against us, as a diagnosis of our defects, and ultimately as a herald of death.

The Law as Measure

The digital revolution has expanded the role of 'metrics' in our lives, whether it be big data or wearable tech that can tell you how many calories you've burned or how well you've slept. Theologians have sometimes compared the Law to a mirror; we can look into a certain idea of perfection, such as a 1600 on the SAT, and see the discrepancy between our ideal selves and our actual selves. We find ourselves being measured, and falling short, all the time. Incomes, test scores, physician's reports, quarterly performance reviews, or criminal records can all give us an approximation of our value in a certain sphere.

The Law acts not only in quantitative metrics, but also in less statistical ways: the gap between who Tom's parents wanted him to be and who he ended up being, the gap between Christianity's central concern for the poor and our own measly giving, the tobacco addiction or browser history or tax fudging or workaholism we simply cannot kick. The Law always accuses, always declares us to be in the wrong. One of the wealthiest men in history (John D. Rockefeller), when asked how much money is enough, replied "Just a little bit more." A famous children's book author once confided that she's terrified her most recent bestseller will be her last. There is no end in sight, and the horizon of what is enough recedes. The author would likely be happier if she could refrain from checking her books' rankings, and could write for the pure joy of the story.

Yet we cannot easily rest with simple doing, or output, but continually desire to have that output evaluated. The allure of measurement is strong: it can tell us that we are making progress and assure of us of definite value. But as football Hall of Famer Woody Hayes once said, "There are only three things that can happen when you throw a pass, and two of them are bad." Stagnation and regression are often the order of the day, and progress remains more elusive than we hope. Furthermore, if and when we do experience real progress, like the children's book author, we feel we must keep it up and fear our best days are behind us. One pastor we know is always terrified his most recent sermon will be his peak, and next Sunday will mark the start of a long decline. Positive feedback only reinforces this fear, by raising the bar of the past and thus setting a higher demand for the future.

When we measure ourselves against the standard of perfection, we generally fall shorter than we'd like. But measures can be manipulated. Practicing money managers, for instance, appear to do extremely well as a group—but largely because the failures have gone out of business and been lost to the record-books. All the young adults in a college town seems beautiful, wealthy, and content—but largely because the burnouts are back home with their parents, the lawbreakers are in jail, and the elderly and frail are sequestered in retirement homes. It's depressing to think about, but it's the real world.

On a smaller scale, we manipulate measures and curate images among families and friends. Tennessee Williams's *Cat On a Hot Tin Roof* gives us the picture of a model Southern family— except the patriarch is dying of cancer and the kids are keeping it a secret; the surface-level friendliness conceals infighting over the soon-to-be-distributed estate; and the virile model son of the family is trapped in a loveless marriage and a downward spiral of alcoholism. Spend a few years pastoring a church (or simply attending one), and the number of families repressing fault-lines and ignoring unpleasant truths becomes astonishing.

In our personal lives, too, we parry any measures which might diagnose our problems. Our career stagnation would suggest we're not that skilled at our job, but we'll choose to believe the boss just has an irrational something against us.[5] Poor Tom was told he was not cut out for a top-tier education by his GPA, a trusted and accurate measure, but his parents spent a good deal of time and money to make the next set of numbers, the SAT, say otherwise. We allow any measure or evaluation to stand as long as it's positive, but otherwise, we massage the facts and construct narratives until they tell us what we want to hear. Again, this problem is not a passive one: We're led into bad decisions and

---

5. Read Arthur Miller's devastating *Death of a Salesman* for an extreme, and heartbreaking, look into this scenario.

situations through systemic overestimation of our own character or ability, also known as hubris.

Behind our need for measures and our selective listening to the truths about ourselves lies an obsession with control. When we hear that all is not well with our desires, our character, and our lives, we rush in to somehow make it well or tell ourselves that everything's okay. When faced with a dose of truth about who we are and what's going on, we desperately desire to be the ones to make it right. To save ourselves.

The Law as Accusation

> "Resolutions? *Me*?? Just what are you implying? That I need to *change*?? Well, Buddy, as far as *I'm* concerned, I'm perfect the way I *am!*"

That's how Calvin responds when his pet tiger Hobbes asks if he is making any resolutions for the new year. Calvin does not hear a question. He hears an accusation, namely, "Your personality could use some work." It's one of the more classic moments in that iconic comic strip (*Calvin and Hobbes*) and, like many that accompany it, contains more than its share of non-cartoon relevance.

We have all had moments where we've heard criticism in the space between words. An innocent question touches on a bruise or insecurity of some kind, and we find ourselves subjecting the inquiring party to a blast of reactivity. An offhand comment about a celebrity—"He sure has lost a lot of weight recently" —is taken personally (translation: *you* haven't), and feelings get hurt.

Other times, though, we are picking up on a critical subtext that's very much there. "Have you seen my keys?," in the context of a marriage, equates to "What did you do with my keys? You're always putting things in strange places (unlike me)."

The irony in the strip is that Calvin's reaction to Hobbes's question reveals just how much he is in need of improvement.

The note of condemnation that he hears, at least in this case, is not a false one. Impetuous and impatient, self-seeking and entitled, Calvin *is* in serious need of betterment. But instead of inspiring fresh resolve, Hobbes's suggestion creates defensiveness, a surefire sign that judgment has been communicated. While this judgment may be well founded, many of the little-l laws we encounter are not. The cultural imperatives about thinness and body image that many teenage girls internalize, for example, are as arbitrary as they are cruel, socially constructed but no less severe than their eternal corollaries. Ideals of beauty shift continually over time—just ask Marilyn Monroe. The accusation endemic to the law of Who You Must Be does not.

God's Law, on the other hand, is a static thing. It tells us what we should do and be in order to live in a peaceful and secure world. The language of the law is usually the language of demand, e.g., words like "should," "ought to," "have to," "must" and "shall." But just because the law often takes the form of an imperative (You must _____) or a command attached to a condition (If you do _____, then you shall live), doesn't mean that it can be boiled down to a grammatical formula—that we can avoid the law simply by avoiding certain words. If only it were so easy!

Indeed, Calvin's response illustrates something crucial. Whether or not an utterance can be called law depends on how it is *heard*, not how it is meant. Law is defined by its effect rather than its intention, and its chief effect is accusation, the intimation of less-than. Which means that in practice, law can be surprisingly elastic. It can just as easily take the form of a statement. For example, "That is the best article you've ever written" may sound like a compliment at first blush, and it is invariably meant as one. Unfortunately, the intention has little bearing on how it is interpreted by its target. There's the immediate second-guessing of "Were the earlier things I've written really bad?" as well as the way that compliments like this, over time, morph into mandate: "Better keep improving and not let people down"—the past looms as a judgment on our present and renders our future precarious.

Such is the nebulous nature of the law that affirmation frequently turns into condemnation. Evaluation is heard as judgment—it doesn't matter if it is positive or negative.[6]

It should come as no surprise, then, that the law cannot be hemmed in by language. A *person* can serve as law in our lives. Think of someone whose very existence represents a judgment on our own: the person from our hometown who had the same basic upbringing and opportunities as us, the same passions and interests, yet whose professional life has been charmed from day one. They just bought their second home, while we just finalized our second divorce.

There are few better or more hilarious pop-culture reference points than one found in the sitcom *Seinfeld*, specifically the relationship of perennially hapless Elaine Benes to her high school rival Sue Ellen Mischke, heiress of the Oh Henry candy bar 'fortune.' The beautiful, confident, effortlessly suave Sue Ellen turns up throughout the series to function as a living comment on everything that Elaine is not—statuesque, beloved, non-neurotic, etc.

What about Sue Ellen, though? As an ostensible law-keeper (of little-l law), does she relate to the command differently from Elaine? The short answer is no. Those who follow the law are, in principle, free from its accusation. The problem is that no one follows the law perfectly—not the little-l laws of society and certainly not the Big-L Law of God (see The Rich Young Ruler, Mk 10:17-22). Ask the most successful person you know about their life, and you'll invariably hear some form of frustration over the truth that the higher you climb, the longer the ladder gets. How

---

6. On the other hand, what sounds like an exhortation to one set of ears may be pure encouragement to another. "You can do better at school" sounds sweet to someone who has never thought of themselves as a student. It sounds caustic to those who have.

else to account for the fact that the most accomplished people feel more, rather than less, pressure to succeed? Or that people who are better looking perceive their blemishes so acutely?

If the law were simply a matter of doing or not doing, commission or omission, we might reasonably imagine we have a shot at keeping it. And sometimes the echoes of law we hear in society are strictly behavioral. Not so with the Law of God. It goes a step further. Christ himself applies the divine ordinance to motivation as well as action. In the Sermon on the Mount, instead of simply prohibiting acts of murder, he prohibits thoughts of murder. Later on he tells us not to worry about *anything*. It turns out he is just as concerned with the inner life as the outer. In his summary of the Law, Jesus even commands us to... love.

Taken together, these imperatives comprise a supremely laudatory code, or godly way of life. A world devoid not only of killing but anger would undoubtedly be a much better one. A world where people loved one another. So the law is not somehow problematic or bad—it is good! The problem is what it exposes in the person who hears it. To wit:

> "The law says, 'Thou shalt love!' It is right; it is 'holy, true, good.' Yet it can't bring about what it demands. It might impel toward the works of the law, the motions of love, but in the end they will become irksome and will all too often lead to hate. If we go up to someone on the street, grab them by the lapels and say, 'Look here, you're supposed to love me!' the person may drudgingly admit that we are right, but it won't work. The results will likely be just the opposite from what our 'law' demands. Law is indeed right, but it simply cannot realize what it points to. So it works wrath. It can curse, but it can't bless. In commanding love law can only point helplessly to that which it cannot produce."[7]

---

7. Gerhard Forde, *On Being a Theologian of the Cross* (Eerdmans, 1997).

The Law that Christ articulates does not ask that we do our best, or that we improve. It is comprehensive. It demands perfection in thought, word, and deed. And because no one is perfect, all stand accused (Rm 3:23). This is why theologians maintain that the Law always accuses. *Lex semper accusat.*

Regardless of how good we feel ourselves to be, how well we think we are doing, or how much better we think we're becoming, there is no getting around the accusation of "Be perfect, as your heavenly Father is perfect" (Mt 5:48). To hear those words clearly is to hear that we are significantly worse off than we imagine ourselves to be—and when it gets down to motivation, even the best things we do have something in them that needs to be forgiven. Moreover, like a husband pointing out the dishes he's done in order to leverage some gratitude from his wife, the second we harness our good deeds for credit is the second they become less good. The motivation becomes self-seeking rather than purely altruistic.

This is not an easy message to accept. After all, it is infinitely easier to defend our actions than our motivations. The former we at least have some modicum of control over, whereas our motivations—both our fears *and* our hopes—are far more slippery. Sharks swim in those waters.

By placing equal emphasis on action and motivation, Christ knocks the wind out of the carefully constructed images we have of ourselves. He demolishes any and all notions of self-sufficiency. We not only stand accused, but condemned. "I fought the law, and the law won" (Bobby Fuller Four).

The Law as Means of Control

If no one fulfills the law, the question naturally arises: Why should we care about it? If it accuses and condemns us—two things that no one likes—why do we pay it such mind? Why does it keep coming back?

Perhaps because the law is a true and good thing. Just because we are not able to live up to God's standard does not somehow invalidate it. That is, we may find it impossible to stop worrying about the future, but that does not mean that less anxiety would be bad. If people were less afraid, the world would undoubtedly be a safer place. No matter how far we've wandered off the path, the 'straight and narrow' is not easily dispensed with, especially when it is inscribed on our conscience (Heb 8:10).

The real reason we cling to the law is more prosaic, though. It has to do with control. Think back to Sunday School (if that's a part of your past), to lessons about gardens and snakes and apples. The portrait of human nature we find in Genesis is of men and women who cannot resist the allure of mastery, who want to be their own Gods. (The serpent's words to Adam and Eve in Genesis 3 are actually "You will be like God.") The grasping for control is the opposite of faith and the essence of original sin, just as it is the essence of our lives. The pursuit of power drives all manner of striving and exhaustion. Conversely, nothing gets people worked up faster than the prospect (or fear) of powerlessness. Spend time in a traffic jam, or in an airport when a flight gets canceled, and this truth becomes self-evident.

So we may dislike being told what to do, we may abhor being criticized, but we *love* being in control. The predilection seems, well, uncontrollable. So, we love the law because it promises us domain—it puts the keys to our wellbeing in our own hands. If I can just do x, y, or z, then I will get the result I want. If I can just be a such-and-such kind of person, or project those qualities publicly, then I will be loved.[8]

---

8. The world of social media often seems tailor-made for illustrations of both how the Law of Who You Must Be manifests itself (exotic vacations, lots of likes, etc.), and how counterproductive those manifestations can be. We edit our personalities and lives online to get the hoped-for response from others—affirmation—and yet, if that response comes, it feels hollow. Because we know the target of the affection is not actually us, just a small sliver of us. Unfortunately we forget that everyone else is dealing with the same dynamic. No surprise that social scientists tell us that the

After all, the law is not just a command, it is a command attached to a *condition*. In the Bible, these conditions are spelled out ('Do/be this and you shall live'). In society, the conditions tend to be implicit, but they're still there ('Do/be this and you'll be lovable, valuable'). The schema varies in specifics but not in its underlying logic: Achievement precedes approval. Behavior precedes belovedness, and so forth. It's no wonder that the lexicon of conditionality—owing, earning, deserving—is baked into our vernacular at a subrational level.

Of course, like the law itself, conditionality isn't *bad*. Some form of *quid pro quo* is necessary. It makes our lives more reliable and less confusing. If you flip the switch, the light will come on. If you don't study hard enough, you will fail the test. This is simply the way things are. We live in a conditional world where actions have consequences.

The problem comes when things don't go as planned, which they never do. When we sleep through our alarm or blurt out an insensitive remark. When our picture ends up in the paper. All of a sudden, the measurements we throw out on our good days boomerang back on our worst. Because for every 'If you do,' there's an 'If you *don't*,' a threat of punishment for every promise of reward. And with threats come resentment, insecurity, and fear, emotions that are often larger than our ability to control them. In these moments, life-management based on conditionality reveals itself to be a dream.

Martin Luther called this condition "The Bondage of the Will," meaning that we are creatures whose decision-making capabilities are fundamentally compromised, and thus we are not free to always fulfill the conditions of success or belovedness. Our wills are distorted so that they desire the wrong things (or the right things for the wrong reasons): as trivial as watching another episode on

---

more time we spend on social media, the happier we perceive our friends to be, and the sadder we feel as a consequence.

Netflix when we know we should be doing laundry, or as serious as cheating on a spouse. "What the heart desires, the will chooses, and the mind justifies" is how one theologian put it. This does not mean that life is pre-determined or that we do not experience choice between, say, oatmeal and cereal, black socks or white. We have a will, it's just not free to choose what is good. That is, no one can, by sheer force of will, resolve to choose the right thing, which is God, *for the right reason,* which is selfless love.

In fact, the truth of why we do the things we do is always far less flattering than our inner optimist would care to admit. The Law will always boomerang back eventually, because "I do not do the good I want, but the evil I do not want is what I do" (Rm 7:19). And the problem goes deeper than traditional misconduct or fear. Even if we wanted to fulfill the law, we *cannot.* Gerhard Forde wrote that we are in "bondage to spiritual ambition, legalism, and tyranny."[9] Nothing shows our lack of freedom better than our addiction to control.

People who are addicted to control—which is all of us, religious or not—are addicted to the law as a means of control. The sad irony of our lives is that our desire to be in control almost always ends up controlling us. For this reason, some would describe our relationship to the law as a fatal attraction.

The Law as Death

The endpoint of the Law is death. This statement needs a lot of unpacking. In the most literal sense, if sin were allowed to run rampant and weren't constrained by criminal penalties, we'd exist in a world of "continual fear, and danger of violent death; and the life of man, solitary, poor, nasty, brutish, and short," as Thomas Hobbes wrote. We're not naturally civil people. Throughout history, we've needed the fear of state-enforced torture, humiliation,

---

9. *Where God Meets Man* (Augsburg Books, 1972). Augustine makes a similar point with 'libido dominandi,' a lust for mastery which masters us.

banishment, imprisonment, or death to keep us straight. Only self-interest keeps all of us from being robbers, killers or rapists. As much optimism as we find in America and elsewhere, the entire order of our world, with its police and prisons and armies and lawyers, is based on the assumption that we're naturally abysmal. Our instinctual behavior leads to death.

Also, death is the judgment God inflicts upon us for our sins. Jesus says that whoever calls someone else a fool will be liable to the fire of Gehenna (Mt 5:22), an awful, smoldering wasteland of "unquenchable fire" (Mk 9:43), where both body and soul could be destroyed (Mt 10:28). Not only will we all die, but also we deserve to die. In fact, the vast majority of Christian theologians have concluded that we deserve not only to die, but afterward deserve a "second death" in Hell, or the "lake of fire," where we would be "tormented day and night forever and ever" (Rev 20:14-15, 10).

While modern-day Christian conservatives believe in original sin and the penalty of death and generally have all their doctrinal ducks in a row, they will quickly self-select out of the depraved category through 'sanctification' and out of the hell category through strong assurance of (their) salvation. And modern-day Christian liberals simply don't talk much about sin and death, viewing evil as less of a personal force and more of a justice problem. It is both: Our sin makes us guilty, and others' sin makes us victims. Sin is writ through our entire world, from fights with your spouse and resentment of your boss to bigotry and systemic oppression. The problem of sin is a problem of self-elevation: Behind individual sins like adultery or greed lies the need to be more-than, to transcend the limits of the flawed, aging, finite people we are. Behind the worst political sins often lies the self-deification of a ruler or caste or nation.[10] Our sense of not being enough and our drive to be more than we are closely intertwine.

---

10. Some of the worst historical cases (French Revolution, Nazism, Stalinism) were underpinned by deeply moralistic ideologies—enlightenment in the former, purity in the latter two, and a sense of Utopian striving in all three.

This self-elevation often brings little non-literal deaths, too. The death of human dignity and cultures, of marriages and friendships. The reality of physical death permeates our lives, sometimes through personal experience of little deaths in suffering, and often through avoidance. We accumulate good works and justify ourselves, whether through careerism or philanthropy, to push away the knowledge that we deserve to die. We build a legacy to outlive us—whether through prestige or influence or over-investing in our children—because we cannot face mortality. People who have hunchbacks or are missing limbs often make us uncomfortable, because we cannot bear to be reminded of how fragile the body is that houses my mind, soul, and identity.

Any genuine religion must face head-on the insurmountable problem of death. One of Christianity's strong points lies in its acknowledgement that we deserve to die, and this is a central problem—perhaps even *the* problem—in our lives, because death negates life utterly. The Law says, 'Do this, and you shall live,' and we fail to 'do this' on a regular basis. The end of sin is death, but the Law, which promises to give us life, also ends in death. As St. Paul wrote, with devastating honesty, "the very commandment that promised life proved to be death to me" (Rm 7:10).

The Law brings death in four ways. First, through God's judgment. Second, in the context above, it may provoke sin, which is associated with death (1 Cor 15:56). The precise mechanism of this is unclear. In Lutheran theology, there's the idea that we are so bound to our desires for freedom and control that a command imposes on our autonomy (etymologically, being a law unto oneself), making us want to *rebel*, to reassert our agency. Try telling a drunk person who's embarrassing himself that it's time to go home: He may have been five minutes from leaving, but suddenly he (fiercely) wants to stay for two more hours. People whose parents were strict on underage drinking may be more likely to go off the rails in college. A book being banned is often a triumph for its marketing. *Fifty Shades of Grey*, a film about

33

sado-masochistic sexuality, benefited from especially high sales in the Bible Belt.[11] The Law incites rebellion, which brings more sin, which brings death. Augustine writes persuasively on this:

> "Yet when the assistance of grace is missing, knowledge of the law is more effective in producing a violation of the commandment. 'Where there is no law, neither is there transgression' [Rm 4:15], says the Apostle... [The Law] commands more than liberates; it diagnoses illness but does not cure. Indeed, far from healing the infirmity, the law actually makes it worse in order to move a person to seek the medicine of grace more anxiously and insistently, because 'the letter kills but the spirit gives life' [2 Cor 3:6]."[12]

Third, the Law—in the more psychological sense of a temptation toward self-reliance—brings death by way of tempting us to depend on ourselves, this time not by rebellion, but a superficial obedience. In the Bible, self-reliance and death are closely associated. In the Garden of Eden, what the serpent described as "being like God" is described by God as "you shall surely die."[13] Behind our attempts to elevate ourselves, either by secular standards or spiritual ones, lies a desire to be more than we are, which kills.[14] For Luther, an even bigger danger than the Law causing rebellion was that of the Law engendering self-righteousness. Sin is self-elevation, and while the Law prohibits certain *manifestations* of that—murder, envy, and the like—it is by no means invulnerable to being co-opted by sinful humans to reinforce the pride and need for control which drives those other symptoms. Again, we thrive on conditionality. For a New Testament example, Jesus

---

11. "All Tied Up in the Bible Belt," *The Economist*, February 14, 2015.

12. *On the Grace of Christ, and on Original Sin*, Book I.

13. For a detailed treatment, see William McDavid, *Eden and Afterward* (Mockingbird, 2014).

14. See too David Zahl's chapter on Michael Jackson from *A Mess of Help* (Mockingbird, 2014).

refers to the Pharisees—the best law-keepers of their day—as "whitewashed tombs" (Mt 23:27). Why the relation between self-reliance, even respectable moral striving, and death?

Beyond the merely physical, biological sense, the word 'life' could be defined as a full experience of the world. Self-reliance narrows this experience, because everything else gets drawn up into the ego's self-propulsion. To be alive means to be open to things outside oneself. We feel truly alive in moments of self-for-getfulness: being transported by a beautiful piece of music, or in moments of love in which we 'lose ourselves' in another. The root of the word 'ecstasy' is the Greek *ek-stasis*: to stand outside, or to be taken out of oneself. To be alive to experience means to be un-self-conscious: The woman who, amidst heaving sobs, pours perfume all over Jesus' feet and wipes them with her hair is someone truly alive. And note the voice of death, from Judas (of all people): "Why wasn't this perfume sold and the money given to the poor?" (Jn 12:6). In human terms, he makes sense here.

If you've been to church regularly, you probably know some-one who is rigidly moral, yet lacks verve, energy, and sponta-neity. It's a common stereotype for the Church in general. We cannot gain life through control and achievement, but those things which we think will give us life actually bring us further into the realm of death. "For those who want to save their life," Jesus said, "will lose it" (Mt 16:25). All of our striving has its end in death—both physical death and ebbing of spirit.

The Law as the Death of the Old Adam

Finally, the Law is the death of the Old Adam. This is awful news, but it brings us to the verge of Good News. In many of the above cases, when law is used as affirmation or a means of control, it speaks indirectly and accuses only obliquely, because each sense of inadequacy or shortcoming it brings is deflected with thoughts like "Next time I'll do better" or "If I try harder, I can make the cut." At issue here is the way we relate to the Law, the question of whether we hear its accusation dead-on or parry it. When the Law functions properly—when it dismantles, rather than provokes, our optimism—it kills the Old Adam.

What do we mean by this? The Old Adam refers to human nature after the Fall. The Old Adam tries to justify himself, tries to be "like God" in the Garden and deceives himself, like the Pharisees, into thinking he's doing 'pretty well.' The Old Adam lives in the world of control, of constant self-measurement and self-reliance. The Old Adam convinces himself, against all empirical evidence to the contrary, that he can make the right decisions. William Ernest Henley, in his poem *Invictus*, wrote the mantra of the Old Adam:

> "I am the master of my fate,
> I am the captain of my soul."

This mindset is extremely burdensome, yet it's largely correct. We all get bad breaks sometimes, or strokes of luck, but our failures are usually ours alone. We may be captains, but we're not good ones. We try so hard to fit the role of the powerful, effective decision-maker. But the reality is different. We have a whole secondary self we put on to deal with circumstance, but inside we are immature, and we know our frailty. Poet Ted Hughes, in a letter to his son, explains this beautifully:[15]

> "Nicholas, don't you know about people this first and most crucial fact: every single one is, and is painfully every moment aware of it, still a child...
>
> It's something people don't discuss, because it's something most people are aware of only as a general crisis of sense of inadequacy, or helpless dependence, or pointless loneliness, or a sense of not having a strong enough ego to meet and master inner storms that come

---

15. Ted Hughes, "Live like a mighty river," *Letters of Note*, http://www.lettersof-note.com/2012/09/live-like-mighty-river.html.

from an unexpected angle. But not many people realise that it is, in fact, the suffering of the child inside them. Everybody tries to protect this vulnerable two three four five six seven eight year old inside, and to acquire skills and aptitudes for dealing with the situations that threaten to overwhelm it. So everybody develops a whole armour of secondary self, the artificially constructed being that deals with the outer world, and the crush of circumstances. And when we meet people this is what we usually meet. And if this is the only part of them we meet we're likely to get a rough time, and to end up making 'no contact'... Usually, that child is a wretchedly isolated undeveloped little being. It's been protected by the efficient armour, it's never participated in life, it's never been exposed to living and to managing the person's affairs, it's never been given responsibility for taking the brunt. And it's never properly lived. That's how it is in almost everybody. And that little creature is sitting there, behind the armour, peering through the slits. And in its own self, it is still unprotected, incapable, inexperienced. Every single person is vulnerable to unexpected defeat in this inmost emotional self. At every moment, behind the most efficient seeming adult exterior, the whole world of the person's childhood is being carefully held like a glass of water bulging above the brim. And in fact, that child is the only real thing in them. It's their humanity, their real individuality... That's the carrier of all the living qualities. It's the centre of all the possible magic and revelation."

The Pharisees were whitewashed tombs because they had invested so much time and energy and effort into building this secondary self, which is the one we see in churches no less than in boardrooms. In observing the secondary self, Hughes was, perhaps unwittingly, describing the Old Adam. And the Law, when it functions properly, exists to destroy and dismantle the armor, leaving the child vulnerable, afraid within.[16] Hughes continues:

> "And so, wherever life takes it by surprise, and suddenly the artificial self of adaptations proves inadequate, and fails to ward off the invasion of raw experience, that inner self is thrown into the front line—unprepared, with all its childhood terrors round its ears."

Just as any honest religion must confront the fact of our death head-on, any honest religion must also address precisely that child, the true self behind the hardened armor of self-justification and adaptation and calculation and coping and control. We may have the illusion of moral self-mastery when Moses tells us not to murder, but what about when Jesus says we'll be liable to hell-fire for insulting someone?

Of course, Jesus did not speak to those with shiny secondary selves, like the Pharisees—except to condemn their righteousness as a lifeless pretension. Instead, the sinners and tax collectors, whose outer armor had long been shorn by addiction and shame and depravity, were the ones to whom Jesus addressed himself. Since only the inner child is truly alive, only that child can hear anything resembling Good News. The secondary self, or the Old Adam, hears only tasks and ways to increase his ego and standing—he only hears in the imperative voice. But the sinner, or inner child, desperately listens for the indicative voice: for some news relevant to his plight. That desperation is the only place an honest approach to the Law can leave us. Yet we still have no Good News, but only a quiet and lonely desperation, now that the illusory capabilities and consolations of the Old Adam are seen to be nothing but "sound and fury, signifying nothing."[17]

---

16. "Suffer little children, and forbid them not, to come unto me: for of such is the kingdom of heaven" (Mt 19:14, KJV).

17. Shakespeare, *Macbeth.*

INTERLUDE: THREE RESPONSES
TO THE LAW

Fight, Flight, Appeasement

The Law, on most every occasion, draws a line of distinction between the *is* of life and the *ought*. The Law is the demarcation of the life we should have—the life we long for—and our own obstructions preventing us from getting there. It is for this reason that our response to the Law is almost always counterproductive.[18]

Imagine you are twelve years old again, and you *love* baseball. All your heroes are baseball players, all your extracurricular time is spent either with a ballglove in hand or watching a game on television, and, regardless of the season, it's been that way as long as you can remember. It's not that you're particularly good or particularly bad at baseball, you just love the game—the smack of the bat after a line drive, the smell of the grass, the feel of sliding headlong into second base. You've never had to defend it or describe it that way, but that's what you feel. And you can imagine one day having a jersey with your name on the back.

---

18. This section draws heavily on "Folly On the Defensive," in chapter 1 of *This American Gospel*, by Ethan Richardson (Mockingbird, 2012).

Things have begun to feel a little different this season, though, because twelve-year-olds have to try out for JV teams at the end of the year, and you get the feeling that not everyone makes the cut. You suddenly find yourself comparing your fielding skills with the other infielders and with players from other teams, and you start to count the number of times you miss balls that are hit to you. You keep track of how many strikeouts you get in each game.

Your coach has a way of calling you out, too. In one particularly bad stretch of the season, your coach calls across the field after you make yet another missed fielding play, "That's four times this game! Keep your head down!" You don't keep your head down, though, and after the fifth ground ball makes its way between your legs, your coach demotes you to the outfield. You replay his voice in your head. At your next at-bat, you strike out quickly, and you wonder if baseball is your sport after all.

The Law is shorthand here for an accusing standard of performance. As we have noted, whenever the Law is coming, condemnation follows close behind. Whenever an expectation stands before us—from our coach, from ourselves, from God himself—we are either condemned by our failure before it, or made to be condemners in our fulfillment of it. The Law is the unfeeling voice of The Coach—it tolerates no excuses, it accepts no shortcuts. The Law is good, in that it proffers good fundamentals ('Keep your head down when fielding a groundball,' 'You shouldn't smoke,' 'Spend only the money you have,' etc.), but the failure which pursues it always creates a reaction. When we are criticized, we must defend.

And how do we defend?

Well, the answer isn't just about Little League pressures; this is the way of life. In facing the Law, we are brought to a moment of internal crisis, where who we are stands in conflict with something we ought to be. In the face of this conflict, one response we tend towards is *flight*. Whether it is the Little League coach, or our spouse, or our super-fit colleague, we run from what someone thinks we ought to be. We think about quitting the team, we disengage emotionally, we stop going to the gym. This reaction to the Law is all about closing our eyes and ears to the sound of our own condemnation. The idea is: We know the problem isn't going anywhere, so we dodge it.

Or perhaps we attempt to assassinate the judge; it's not flight, it's *fight*. We put up our dukes and argue our case with the Coach, even if we know it will relegate us to the bench. We rationalize our decisions and the mistakes we made—how they weren't even mistakes at all. We bicker on our job surveys about unrealistic expectations, we condescend about the vanity of the kinds of people who go to the gym, and we blame our parents for what they've done to us. In one way or another, this is our approach: to turn the speakers up in rebellion against the unfairness of an overly harsh Coach.

Or maybe we *appease*. The Coach isn't satisfied, so we show him how sorry we are, how hard we've been practicing at home. Our skills are bound to improve if He just gives us time. We ingratiate ourselves in the hopes that the Law might be appeased. We decide to wear what they wear, instead of what we want to wear; we apologize needlessly for fear that people are always mad at us; we go to the gym from time to time, and justify why we don't go more often. More or less, we cower before judgment, hoping to sneak some sympathy in before the bite.

It must be mentioned that this is true for our spiritual lives, too. We become master minimizers of God's call for perfection. We tend to lower the bar of God's righteous Law, in the hopes that fulfilling one or a small set of them will be enough to gain the Almighty's ear. Of course, it's impossible to keep all of the Bible's various moral teachings before us at any one time. Selectivity is a foregone conclusion, and the criteria for such selection will always be pride-driven, at least in part. But it is also a defense mechanism, dividing up righteousness into manageable, seemingly do-able parts. Like the Rich Young Ruler who walks away from Jesus in great sadness, we'd certainly like to parse and snip our way into an achievable spirituality—one that doesn't drive us to the grave every day of our lives.

But, in fact, that is precisely what the Law does. We can only react so long until our reactions are silenced. As we are told in scriptures, "Behold, you have sinned against the Lord, and be sure your sin will find you out" (Nm 32:23).

THE GOSPEL

News from Across the Sea

'News' expresses something different from 'knowledge.' We live in a time of unprecedented knowledge: a day's worth of new data now would be, in terms of raw amount of information, the envy of entire centuries past. Knowledge equips us to better live in the world around us: The scientist must be in control in the lab, and the factory manager needs good data on her employees' output, the cost of raw materials, and the reliability of her machinery. This kind of 'hard' knowledge is crucial to our ability to manage our lives and adapt to the world we live in.

The Catholic writer Walker Percy took issue with our myopic focus on knowledge in an essay titled "The Message in the Bottle."[19] Adapting to and managing our world is a good thing, but we are more than simply detached scientists or statisticians. He uses the example of logicians at a meeting: If someone ran in and yelled, "Fire!" they would immediately run out of the building *before* carefully studying the sentence. For a moment, the accumulation of knowledge is no longer the most important thing. News is. The chance that the logicians might be in a plight

---

19. From *The Message in the Bottle* (New York: Picador, 2000).

which threatens their existence dwarfs all else, and they respond accordingly.

Percy envisioned a castaway who, in his plane crash or boat accident, loses his memory of the past. The castaway washes up onshore of an advanced island civilization, and he spends his days walking on the beach, where thousands of bottles with messages in them wash up every day. Some messages, like "The pressure of a gas is a function of heat and volume," are easily tested and, if true, may lead to major advances in machinery or understanding of the world. Other messages, like "Jane will arrive tomorrow," are not knowledge, but news.

News, in Percy's example, is something which cannot be discovered or easily tested by the scientist, or by anyone else. It will not add much to the store of human knowledge, and often, as probably in this case, it is totally insignificant. But news is defined by its peculiar relation to the well-being of the hearer. When the castaway reports Jane's imminent arrival to the islanders, some may be curious, but many will be more excited about the scientific breakthrough in their understanding of gases. Still, there may be one man somewhere on the island for whom this announcement means everything, the man who was married to a woman named Jane before she left years ago on a canoe, never to be seen again. This man will be thrown into a state of utter joy, mixed perhaps with anticipation and frustration and anxiety, about this visitor.

Again, we see that news, depending on the hearer, may be infinitely more significant than knowledge. The latter equips the secondary self, the one who adapts to and manages the world, but the former may address the inner man behind the armor. The predicament of the hearer matters.

Returning to our castaway, Percy says that though he "may or may not be an objective-minded man," he also may "find himself in a certain predicament." For example, if he is thirsty, the sentence "There is fresh water in the next cove" will not be filed away with other assertions to test, but it will take on a direct personal significance. The sentence may not even be true—let's say only about one in every ten messages in the bottles is true—but if he is near death from thirst, he will give up all else and walk to the next cove.

Knowledge is a matter of truth and untruth, whereas *news* may be improbable, wild, even absurd. Yet if it has a direct bearing on the plight of the hearer, he will listen. Percy's castaway thrives on the island, but all is not well:

> "But if we say to him only that something is very wrong and that after fifty years on the island he is still a stranger and a castaway, he must listen, for he knows this better than anyone else.
>
> Then what should he do? It is not for me to say here that he do this or that or should believe such and such. But one thing is certain. He should be what he is and not pretend to be somebody else. He should be a castaway and not pretend to be at home on the island. To be a castaway is to be in a grave predicament and this is not a happy state of affairs. But it is very much happier than being a castaway and pretending one is not. This is despair. The worst of all despairs is to be at home when one is homeless.
>
> But what is it to be a castaway? To be a castaway is to search for news from across the seas."

All the knowledge and skills in the world—which might help him grow his business, be a better father, make contributions to history and economics and science and medicine, and distinguish himself—will not address what he feels, deep down, to be "very wrong." He is still a castaway, and still homeless.

The entire time, of course, Percy's clever polemic against our culture's obsession with empirical knowledge is tracing the shape of faith, carving out a place for it alongside knowledge. In his parable, the Law is operating by pricking the castaway with a sense of uneasiness, the sense that something is amiss. When the Law is *preached*, that is, and the pastor *connects with the hearer's particular plight*—then he must listen. Our inner child, flailing and alone, will know to search for news relevant to her 'existential plight,' or the troika of guilt, death, and meaninglessness. Christ said, "Those who are well have no need of a physician, but those who are sick; I have come to call not the righteous but sinners" (Mk 2:17). The righteous cannot recognize Christ, because they are pretending they are not castaways; they are unaware of their predicament and thus blind to the News which addresses it. But the sinners and outcasts and poor, those who know they are castaways, take to Christ immediately.

The Gospel is News not only because it addresses our plight, but also because it comes wholly from outside of ourselves. It is not something we could have discovered, invented, or imagined. It is news because it is *new*. It arrives from beyond the boundaries of our ego, beyond all we know. It is news from across the seas, from the other side of the unbridgeable gulf between humans and God. It is "wholly Other," as theologian Karl Barth said. And it is *Good* News because it addresses our plight with *rescue, deliverance, salvation,* and *redemption*. It may not empower us, may not help the advance of civilization or give us more control over our world. But it addresses our plight and proclaims that we have been delivered.[20]

News About a Person

It is vital that the news comes from somewhere external to us. A broken machine cannot fix itself nor, as theologian Rudolf Bultmann once observed, can someone sinking in a swamp pull himself out by tugging upward on his own hair. Knowledge

---

20. People sometimes speak of 'living the Gospel' or 'Gospel in action.' But this would be a 'category mistake,' a failure to see the new *as new*. The Law may be acted out by us, but the Gospel is received.

relates to and empowers the self, which helps the self solve the everyday problems and hurdles it faces. But when the problem *is* the self, help must come from outside: must be News that we cannot manipulate (because we would botch it), but is *objectively* true. But how can something so beyond our normal ways of doing and acting be communicated?

If Earth were facing destruction and no one had any way to avoid it, an advanced, benevolent alien civilization might send a message. But we could not decode it; their language is far beyond our own. Perhaps an alien might even study English, immerse himself in what, to him, is a simplistic language. But say the message—for instance, "Do this...and you shall live"—were something we simply could not follow? Perhaps we are given two thousand years to heed their advice, and though we worship the aliens as deliverers of our doomed world, we continue to contradict their wisdom. Things only get worse.

At that point, the aliens might decide to send an emissary. He is humble, and he comes in human form. Because he's still an alien, he interprets and understands the aliens' words—collected, after two thousand years, in a sacred book—better than everyone else, though he's had little education. He shows impatience with those who think they understand the aliens' advice but do not, and he loves those who are wretched, those who make the world a worse place by their actions and are miserable themselves. They alone see something special about this alien-person, so pariahs and scoundrels flock to him. The written advice has failed them, so they're looking not for another command or more advice but for *news*. Sadly, his message is too strange and, well, alien to the normal human ways of doing things. He's too critical of the alien-worshipping elite, and eventually he's killed as a threat to order.[21]

---

21. See too Mt 21.

This point of this rather long-winded parable is that *news is not command*. Command comes in the imperative voice—'Do this'—and news comes in the indicative voice—'This has been done.' But this News is more than words. Mere words do not work, because they're addressed to sinners, who misunderstand and manipulate them. Centuries after the good alien is killed, his words will be used to justify tyranny, to baptize massacres, to torture people into paying the good alien lip service.

Which is perhaps why Christ—not an alien, but *God himself*—seemed, on some level, not to *want* people to know who he was, instructing those he'd healed to tell no one, and ordering his disciples, once they finally realized who he was, to keep silent about it. He seemed more concerned with personal presence than reputation or even clear teaching (Mk 4:12). Words can be dodged and manipulated and misused. The Law consists of words, but the *Gospel is a Person*. This is one reason Jesus was called the "Word of God"—because God's entire revelation to humans *is* this Person.

Signs and wonders and displays of power were not Christ's way of doing things. Contrary to how humans operate, *God's glory is seen in his condescension*, his downward movement toward earthlings.[22] Christ is marked first by his humility and self-abasement, his downward trajectory. So it takes special "eyes to see" this person, special "ears to hear" his message, as it is so counter-intuitive.[23]

This Person is certainly 'news from across the sea,' from beyond the planet and beyond the impassable divide between Creator and creation. He is God incarnate, yet a carpenter's apprentice. He accumulates no wealth or power, beyond the

---

22. This idea has been most fully developed by J.G. Hamann.

23. Martin Luther made a contrast between the "Theology of the Cross," which finds God's glory in the least and the lost, or in what often appears foolish to humans; and the "Theology of Glory," which searches for God in what is wise or strong by worldly standards. See Luther's *Heidelberg Disputation*, readable at bookofconcord.org, for more.

occasional veneration of riffraff and mobs, who are mainly in it for bread or healing or a chance at a nationalistic figurehead to push the Romans out of town. He says and does odd things, like giving teachings almost meant to baffle rather than enlighten, or describing God's coming kingdom as something hidden, paradoxical, and outrageous.[24] He dies a humiliating traitor's death, like that of an ordinary outlaw. He tells a criminal being crucified beside him that "today you will be with me in paradise," a tragic and farcical thing coming from a dying, failed rabbi whose life has come to naught. Before expiring, he cries to God the Father, perplexed at his desertion, "My God, my God, why have you forsaken me?" and then dies. Three days later, he comes back to life—vindicating the trust which sinners and fishermen had placed in him. He does some teaching, cooks some breakfast, maybe fishes a little, and then disappears. Two thousand years later, we're still trying to come to grips with him.

The Good News is a Person who accomplishes our deliverance. Between God's assumption of a human form, Jesus' crucifixion, and his resurrection, *something* very good has happened: Something, some "*it*," "is finished" (Jn 19:30).

What did God do on earth; what does this Person mean? A few years after Jesus' death, a model citizen and perfect lawkeeper named Saul is on his way to Damascus to continue his campaign against this new, irreverent, and blasphemous sect of Judaism when he is visited by its founder and blinded, a symbol for how blind he himself had been to God in human form. After changing his name to Paul, he begins to reflect on Christ's life and teachings. Aided by the Holy Spirit, he decides it means several things: First, God has broadened his reach beyond the Jews to the entire world. Second, our sins are forgiven, and the powers of death, the Law, and sin over us have been broken. Third, we are given new lives, lives which do not operate by the old conditionality and

---

24. Nod to Robert Farrar Capon's fantastic *Kingdom, Grace, Judgment*.

self-mastery or even moralism, but by the Spirit and by freedom. The Old Adam has been supplanted by a New one: "If anyone is in Christ, there is a new creation" (2 Cor 5:17).

There is a gap between Paul and Jesus: Jesus taught mainly about the coming Kingdom of God, but Paul writes mainly about grace and forgiveness and reconciliation with God. One easy maxim to lessen the tension is to note that "Paul taught what Jesus did."[25] But this gap is important to keep in mind. If we focus only on Jesus' life, we find him to be a moral example, a figure of love, or a healer to be emulated. But Paul tells us how to read Jesus' life, how to see him accomplishing a radical act of Good News. If Christ is Good News, then Paul is the divinely-sanctioned analyst of it.

At the same time, it is dangerous to focus solely on Paul and neglect the Man himself. The statements, 'You are forgiven' or 'You are loved unconditionally' are by themselves only sentimental, airy and abstract statements with little grounding in reality. Their point of connection with our world is in the life and actions of the Person who lived in our history, who walked dusty roads and ate and drank and got indigestion, someone who experienced the setbacks and challenges of daily life, yet was sinless. The Gospel is not mere forgiveness or grace, empty of content, but always refers to Jesus.

So the Gospel is Good News, about a human Person who is God in our history, our world, and who came to accomplish *something* in his life, death, and resurrection. That 'something' is not only news from across the sea, but also a gift from above.

The Gift that Never Stops Giving

There is no more subversive song than "Santa Claus Is Coming to Town." But it's not subversive for the reasons that religious

---

25. Paul Zahl. One of his books, *The First Christian*, addresses this tension head-on.

people usually take issue with Santa, when they lament the commercialization and 'secularization' disguised in the detour from Bethlehem to the North Pole. No, that holiday classic is so subversive on account of how effectively it sabotages the beating heart of Christmas, which has to do with giving.[26]

We tell children that Santa Claus comes down the chimney to deliver them presents. To shower them with gifts. The song paints a different picture: "He's making a list/ He's checking it twice/ He's gonna find out/ who's naughty and nice." Nice children get toys, naughty ones lumps of coal. This Santa Claus is not actually a giver of gifts. He's in the business of doling out reward and punishment.

As we all know, any gift premised on deserving is not really a gift at all. It's more of a paycheck, an act based in reciprocity rather than generosity. A gift, on the other hand, is a decidedly lopsided transaction, and therefore a fitting image for Christmas, which marks the remembrance of Christ's birth.

The baby Jesus represents *pure* Gift, a light shining on those who dwell in darkness, the revelation of God's love in all its vulnerability and impossibility. Like all true gifts, he arrives unbidden—a great and glorious surprise, a savior given to those who don't deserve one. As the one who will "save people from their sins" (Mt 1:21), the Christ child signifies something startlingly new and unassailably good.

In his life and ministry, Christ would bear out this divine generosity. He would become a walking euphemism for it. Again, those who welcomed him most enthusiastically would be they whose lives had stripped them of any illusions about deservedness, a.k.a. sinners. Their *only* way of receiving him was as a gift. This is what we see in Christ's treatment of lepers and tax collectors and prostitutes and reprobates—he does not relate to

---

26. Let's not blame Santa himself for what the song has wrought. Clement Moore introduced the popular version of St. Nick in 1823 with "Twas the Night Before Christmas" but "Santa Claus is Coming to Town" didn't come onto the scene until 1934.

them on the basis of what they bring to the table but on the basis of who he is. And it makes every difference. He is the 'Yes' to the world's 'No' (2 Cor 1:20).

Jesus praises children for this very reason; their inability to earn is not up for debate. They are powerless, and consequently have yet to turn love into a bartering system. Indeed, the strongest resistance Christ encounters comes from those who insist on paying for what is offered freely, who refuse to give up their rights—the place they feel their sweat has earned them on the Listmaker-in-the-Sky's scorecard.

Though the law is conditional—a two-way street—the gift of Christ is unconditional. His affection cannot be leveraged or merited. This is what we mean when we talk about the attitude of grace, which is one-way love, or 'love in the midst of deserved judgment.' Jesus simply gave—his attention, his power, his very self—and to the wrong people. This is why Robert Capon wrote, "Grace works without requiring *anything* on our part. It's not expensive. It's not even cheap. It's free."[27]

Most things in life are complicated, but this is not one of those things. Something is either a gift or a wage—it can't be a little of each (Rm 5:15). The moment that a price or condition enters the equation, it is no longer a gift, no longer grace. This applies to present-tense conditions just as much as future-tense ones. If a friend gives us a car for example, out of the blue, most of us would pause before accepting. We appreciate the gesture perhaps, but what's the catch? Is our friend 'buying' our loyalty (and what does that say about our friendship)? Is there an unspoken expectation that we'll do a favor-in-kind some day? Are we in *Godfather* territory? We harbor a kneejerk suspicion of the excessively generous, and for good reason. There's no such thing as a free lunch. A present with strings attached is a bribe, not a gift.

---

27. *The Romance of the Word: One Man's Love Affair with Theology* (Eerdmans, 1996).

Of course, even if we're able to welcome the Gift when it comes *our* way, we are considerably less excited when we see it extended to others, especially those who have done us wrong in some way. Grace, it turns out, is fundamentally unfair and therefore offensive—it makes no allowance for what we feel we, or anyone else, are owed. Which hints at why Christ encountered such profound opposition to his ministry, ending in his execution. Human nature is such that we may appreciate the gift in theory but not so much in practice. A pure gift upsets the balances of power. It may even invert them. Unconditional love is so threatening to sinful men and women and the precious hierarchies they create, that the one time it was made fully manifest in history, we killed it.[28]

You might say, then, that the chief 'offense' of the Gospel has nothing to do with morality. It has to do with control being wrenched out of our clutching hands, with the last being first and the first last. Brennan Manning summed it up beautifully when he wrote in his memoir, *All Is Grace*:

> "My life is a witness to vulgar grace—a grace that amazes as it offends. A grace that pays the eager beaver who works all day long the same wages as the grinning drunk who shows up a ten till five. A grace that hikes up the robe and runs breakneck toward the prodigal reeking of sin and wraps him up and decides to throw a party no ifs, ands, or buts. A grace that raises bloodshot eyes to a dying thief's request—"Please, remember me"—and assures him, "You bet!" A grace that is the pleasure of the Father, fleshed out in the carpenter Messiah, Jesus the Christ, who left His Father's side not for heaven's sake but for our sakes, yours and mine. This vulgar grace is indiscriminate compassion."[29]

---

28. Fortunately, we are not left to our own devices. If the resurrection of Christ tells us anything, it's that nothing can stop the love of God—not our virulent opposition, not even the judgment of the grave.

29. From chapter 19.

Needless to say, the reality of God's grace is so radical that we often find ourselves trying to domesticate it, unconsciously (or not), imposing all manner of fine print about what constitutes acceptance or rejection. We pontificate about the proper response to the Gift, as if God is subject to our code of manners. At Christmas, for example, what if you forget to send a thank-you note immediately? What if, when you do, it's a fairly shabby piece of work? What if you never send one? Will the gift be revoked? Again, any gift premised on the recipient's 'correct' response to it is not much of a gift at all. Indeed, as most married couples can attest, the more pressure we place on the recipient to react a certain way, the less likely they are to do so.

The friendship analogy can help us here as well, since of the most common ways we divest the Gift of its purity, and reintroduce the law, is by jumping too hastily into 'relationship' territory. While there is indeed a sense in which the Gift invites its recipient into dialogue (such as prayer, thanksgiving, confession, etc.), our tit-for-tat programming is so strong that it tends to hijack the beauty of grace, and instead position it conditionally. Which makes sense. Even our closest relationships on Earth have some element of give-and-take—how could we not project that dynamic onto our Heavenly Father? 'He did everything for me, now it's time for me to do something for him,' or so the thinking goes. Yet obligation yields guilt, and guilt creates distance. Soon we're not returning his calls.

Fortunately, while Christ relates to us, he is not us. He is unfazed by our protestations and reversions. He can handle our inner Santa Claus. No amount of fearful insistence on recompense can make *this* gift any less of one (Jn 21). We do not possess the power to invalidate divine generosity, or renegotiate the terms of our acceptance. The Giver is good and so is the Gift.

Forgiveness

If Christ is the Gift of God, what is it that he imparts? In giving himself, what are we receiving? This has been the subject of fierce debate over the centuries, a profound and important question but not an unanswerable one, at least partially. Let us take our cue from St. Paul:

> "In [Christ] we have redemption through his blood, the forgiveness of sins, in accordance with the riches of God's grace." (Ephesians 1:7)

> "He was delivered over to death for our sins and was raised to life for our justification." (Romans 4:5)

> "He has rescued us from the power of darkness and transferred us into the kingdom of his beloved Son, in whom we have redemption, the forgiveness of sins." (Colossians 1:13-14)

If we take these verses at face value, Paul seems to be identifying three elements of what we are given in Christ: the forgiveness and absolution of sins, the justification of sinners, and citizenship in his kingdom.

First, the forgiveness of sins. It's impossible to read the Gospel accounts and miss the centrality of forgiveness in the ministry of Christ. In fact, he seems to regard forgiveness as the most pressing need of human beings, above even that for healing (Mk 2:1-12). And not just one-time forgiveness, but ongoing, limitless forgiveness (Mt 18:22).

It is a bold claim, but given the amount of scar tissue we carry around from past wrongdoing—other people's and our own—perhaps not as far-fetched as it might initially sound.[30]

---

30. Perhaps you've met someone who can't stand the idea of needing to be forgiven, someone for whom forgiveness implies the sort of guilt about "who we are" that traumatizes so many children growing up in religious households. Ironically, those tend to be situations marked by an *absence* of forgiveness rather than an abundance of it. Even in these extreme cases, though, while there might be re-

Forgiveness occupies an equally central place in life as it does in theology. Its presence saves lives. Its lack destroys them.

Furthermore, we can probably all agree that true forgiveness is rare, the exception rather than the rule in human affairs. When sinned against, we prefer holding grudges to turning the other cheek. We opt for litigation, revenge, comeuppance. That is, we opt for law over grace. Just watch any episode of any reality TV show ever. Even in those cases where we may want to forgive another person, we find that it is seldom a simple act of willpower. The injunction to forgive may be a good and noble command, but it cannot inspire us to do so. As much as we may need forgiveness, we cannot seem to generate it. Emily Dickinson was on to something when she wrote, "the Heart with the heaviest freight on— / Doesn't— always— move—"

Enter Jesus Christ. He did more than simply advocate for mercy, he actively embodied it. As a third party, i.e., not the one sinned against, it would have been audacious for him to presume he could grant anything resembling pardon—unless, of course, he had some special authority, which he claimed to have. "Against you, you alone, have I sinned" (Ps 51:4). Christ was (and is) more than a vehicle of mercy; he was Mercy itself.

Much as we might wish it were not the case, for forgiveness to be believable and efficacious, there has to be some basis for it. Say you borrow a friend's phone to make an important call. It's an animated conversation, and the device mistakenly slips from your grasp and falls into the street, where, before you can pick it up, a car runs it over. These things happen, your friend tells you, totally understandable. Just grab me a new one, and we're good. When you hand him the new phone the next day, he gives you a hug. All is forgiven. And you believe it in a way you wouldn't if he had just shrugged it off.

---

luctance about universalizing, it takes an equally extreme willfulness to maintain that there is nothing—not a single thing—for which they would like to be forgiven. There is nothing more despair-inducing in relationships than blamelessness.

Author and shame researcher Brené Brown touched on this dynamic in a more visceral way when she talked about coming back to church after years away and the moment "the whole Jesus thing" finally clicked:

> "People would want love to be unicorns and rainbows. So then you send Jesus, and people say, 'Oh my god, love is hard, love is sacrifice, love is trouble, love is rebellious.' As Leonard Cohen sings, 'Love is not a victory march/ It's a cold and it's a broken hallelujah.' Love isn't hearts and bows. It is very controversial.
>
> In order for forgiveness to really happen, something has to die. Whether it's your expectations of a person, or your idea about who you are. There has to be a death for forgiveness to happen. In all of these faith communities where forgiveness is easy, and love is easy, there's not enough blood on the floor to make sense of that."

All of a sudden, it becomes clear why Christians take the forgiveness of sins to heart. The blood on the floor is Christ's own.

Modern sensibilities understandably find something gruesome about this notion of blood atonement, something noxious and reductively economic about the concept of propitiation. But think about your own life for a moment. Debits, credits, penalties, bonuses, etc.—these factors are seemingly hardwired into the human brain, and they operate independent of ideology. 'I reached out last time. Now it's her turn.' 'If you hurt me, there must be an apology before things are copacetic.' For reconciliation to occur, a cost has to be paid, a condition met—'Either you say you're sorry, I swallow my pride, or we go our separate ways.' It's the way the world works even beyond human relationships, which is one reason why the Hebrew Scriptures are so concerned with animal sacrifice. The law will not be ignored.[31]

---

31. There are other ways of understanding atonement: For example, Paul also talks about being "united" to Christ in his death, and looking forward to sharing in his resurrection (Rm 6). This idea of union in Christ's death expresses some-

Likewise the transgression (and exploitation) of God's Law, the refutation of God's authority, is no small thing. The resulting crimson stain cannot simply be wished away. Something has to *happen* to bring sinners into accord with their creator—for us to trust that forgiveness is not theoretical but concrete. That God would condescend to us in history in a way that both acknowledges and resolves these fundamental realities is not juvenile or overly abstract—it is both miraculous and merciful, evidence that we are both fully known and fully loved. Again, the Law commands that we love perfectly. The Gospel announces that we are perfectly loved.

What about the violence involved? How do we square the crucifixion of Christ with a loving God? It's not always easy. But perhaps the extreme nature of the 'solution' points to the extreme nature of the predicament. The crucifixion is not an excessive act of 'divine child abuse' so much as the unmistakable picture of a savior who gives his life for those he came to redeem, the same ones who could not abide the audacity of his indiscriminate compassion. Where some see (anthropomorphized) cruelty, we might see the opposite: "the Lamb of God who takes away the sins of the world" (Jn 1:29). Meaning, the love of God is not just any love. It is love made manifest in self-sacrifice and willful substitution, one for all and once for all time.

Importantly, we speak not only of the forgiveness of sins, but their absolution. This radicalizes the Gift further: Our misdeeds are not just pardoned but *erased*. "As far as the east is from the west, so far does he remove our transgressions from us" is how the Psalmist puts it (Ps 103:12). The slate is more than clean—it's brand new, perpetually so.

Paul Zahl likens absolution to "divine amnesia," and it runs directly counter to a culture where technology has made our

---

thing important about how Christ's death is the end of the Old Adam, and the new man is raised up by God.

every misstep or lapse in judgment searchable and permanent. You don't have to be an ex-con to find yourself beholden to a rap-sheet long after the sentence has been served, the debt paid. Your infractions are out there for anyone with an Internet connection to find. Politicians talk of "the right to be forgotten" and wonder how such a thing could ever be possible with a scorekeeping species. The bad news is that it's not. The good news is that what's impossible with man is possible with God. "Are you washed in the blood of the lamb?" goes the American spiritual, and while the language may ring slightly archaic, the words will never lose their meaning or appeal.

Of course, in those places where the Gospel speaks loudest we inevitably find ourselves grasping most desperately for the law. How does this happen in regard to forgiveness? Our tactic is somewhat diagonal. We make 'repentance' a pre-condition for pardon. We insist that people express remorse before we let them off the hook. In this scenario, sorrow somehow activates absolution.

This not only undercuts the gravity of Christ's promises—if they are subject to our ever-shifting attitudes, how trustworthy can they be?—it opens up a rabbit hole of introspection and second-guessing. You said you were sorry, but did you *mean* it? And if you really meant it, why did you do the same thing a week later? Human behavior is back to being the key that unlocks divine favor. Fortunately, all our carefully curated testimonies and feebly drawn portraits of personal progress cannot shake Calvary's foundation.

If the Gospel is really to be Good News, forgiveness must find its grounding outside of us, which it does, in the death and resurrection of Christ. This is why sinners like us are bold enough to say that God forgives *before* we have the chance to come clean (Rm 5:8). In fact, that happy news may even give us the freedom and fearlessness to realize just how much we need to do so.

All this said, there may be something presumptuous about claiming to understand the exact mechanics of cosmic reconciliation. If we could, it probably wouldn't be divine or complete. The backstory, or cause, of the forgiveness of sins has power, but to the one drowning in a sea of trouble, the only thing that matters is the outstretched hand—not the physics of salvation, but salvation itself.

Perhaps it is enough to say that the Law reveals that we need to be forgiven; the Gospel announces we have been forgiven. Full stop.

Justification

Forgiveness is only part of what we are given in Christ. Paul invokes another term, a legal one: justification. To justify someone means to make or declare them righteous, 'in the right.' Being cleared of wrongdoing and being vindicated are parts of what it means to be justified.

"If you live in America in the 21st century you've probably had to listen to a lot of people tell you how busy they are," essayist Tim Kreider famously observed, pinpointing one of the most inescapable pathologies of modern life. When asked how we are doing, we used to say, 'fine' or 'well.' Today the default response is 'busy.' Which is an honest answer. Smartphones and similar devices have largely chased away the uncomfortable idleness that once characterized society, quickening the pace of life to an almost absurd degree. People *are* busy. We are busy. Very busy.

But 'busyness' is more than a description of how we're doing; it is one of our culture's predominant indicators of worth and value, a measure of identity and therefore personal righteousness. The more frantic the activity, the better. Kreider spelled this out when he theorized that, "busyness serves as a kind of existential reassurance, a hedge against emptiness; obviously your life cannot possibly be silly or trivial or meaningless if you are so busy, completely booked, in demand every hour of the day."

What does it say about you if you're not busy? Nothing good, so get back on the horn. The implication is that if we're not over-occupied, we are inferior to those who are. As with all law-based barometers of self-worth (beauty, wealth, influence, youth, etc.), there is no 'enough.'[32] Any justification we may attain through exertion is short-lived to say the least.

What the near-universal obsession with busyness reveals is that *everyone* is religious, not just those who believe in God or go to church. Everyone worships. Everyone is trying to earn their salvation. 'Works righteousness'—the attempt to justify yourself by works of the law (be they actions or attributes)—is the default mode of *human* operation, not just the select few who identify as religious. The law reigns over all creation; the question is not if but which form a person subscribes to.

'Performancism' is a helpful way to describe what it looks like to justify ourselves. In a performancist paradigm, there is no distinction between our résumé and our identity. Our performance—in whatever realm we value most—is not just descriptive of us, it *is* us. It might be a bank balance or a weight scale, church attendance records or college admissions results, but if you are not doing (and doing well), your very life is at stake, to say nothing of your dignity or wellbeing.

A performancist mindset is one ensconced in law and the dread and exhaustion it produces. Wherever you are most tired, look closely and you'll likely find self-justification at work.

The Gospel announces that we are justified by grace through faith: not by what we do, or even who we are, but by what Christ has done and who he is. Our guilt has been atoned for, the Law fulfilled. In Christ, the ultimate demand has been met, and the deepest judgment satisfied. In his death and resurrection, our sin

---

32. See also *The Onion*'s classic headline "Fully Validated Kanye West Retires to Quiet Farm in Iowa."

was imputed to him, his righteousness to us. Note the past tense: This is not up for grabs. Something has been accomplished, and that something is total. Remember, Christ's dying words from the cross are "It is finished." Which means that as far as God is concerned, the performance is at an end—gold stars all around. This leads to reconciliation with God, and even to eternal life: "For if while we were enemies, we were reconciled to God through the death of his Son, much more surely, having been reconciled, will we be saved by his life" (Rm 5:10).

Finally, we have become God's people. In the Hebrew Scriptures, citizenship was based primarily on ethnicity. Now, it is based on the blood of Jesus and what he has done. This is powerful because it sheds light on St. Paul's concept of being ambassadors for Christ. We do not come up with our own message, but instead we simply declare the message that God has given us. The struggle between us and God is now over. We are his children and citizens of this eternal kingdom. For now, we cannot help but live a little bit like the soldiers in the final battles of the Civil War, which took place months after the South had surrendered. Those fighting on had not yet received the word that the war was over.

In a life governed by the Law, striving for victory and fear of defeat loom over every endeavor. In a life governed by the Gospel, *nothing that needs to be done hasn't already been done.* Or as Martin Luther so famously wrote in thesis 23 of the Heidelberg Disputation (1518), "the law says 'do this,' and it is never done. Grace says, 'believe in this' and everything is already done." We have nothing to lose or gain, in other words. The pressure to self-justify has been removed, whether we believe it or not, and it has been replaced with freedom: the freedom to die and yet to live, to fail and yet succeed. The freedom to play, to serve, to love, to wait, to laugh, to cry, to sit idle—even to get busy.

Yes, judgments against us will persist just as sin persists, but the Gospel pronounces that these judgments have lost their bite.

The law has been defanged. The condemnation we feel is simply a feeling, no more binding than any other. So we may judge others, and they may judge us; we may judge ourselves, but God has gotten out of the judgment game. Christ is the final word on that score. This is not just good news. It is the *best* news.

FRUITS OF THE GOSPEL

The Gospel has been known to produce fruit in the lives of those who take it to heart. These are characteristics of people who know themselves to be free from the Law and saved through grace, as a result of Christ. St. Paul speaks of the "fruits of the Spirit" as being love, joy, peace, patience, kindness, generosity, faithfulness, gentleness, and self-control (Gal 5:22-23). These are important and natural outgrowths of the Spirit's presence in the lives of believers, but here we're just going to speak about 'fruits of the Gospel'—immediate effects of the message of justification, such as humility and gratitude. Of course, these two qualities would lead someone to be more patient, kind, and gentle, so we're hoping the Spirit's fruits still get their due. But the list of traits below—humility, receptivity, gratitude, spontaneity, humor, freedom, and comfort—tries to both encapsulate Paul's fruits and give some less Sunday-School fruits their due.

Language about 'fruits' is dangerous, though, because as sinners we are tempted to examine our own lives for signs of these fruits. Of course, once we're evaluating ourselves, we're squarely back to the territory of Law.[33] Needless to say, we often become discouraged when we find that we're the same old people. Rod

---

33. And alongside it, pride, control, sin, and/or despair.

Rosenbladt, a Lutheran theologian, summed up well the discouragement this can produce:

> "Think of the inner soliloquy many Christians experience week by week: 'There may have been grace for me when, as a sinner, I was initially converted. But now, having been given the Spirit of God, I fear that things have gotten worse in me rather than better. I have horribly abused all of God's good gifts to me. I was so optimistic in the beginning, when the pastor told me that Christ outside of me, dying for me, freely saved me by his death, and that the Holy Spirit now dwelling within me would aid me in following Christ... I have rededicated myself to Christ more times than I can count. But it seems to stay the same, or even get worse, no matter what I do. Whatever the outer limits of Christ's grace are, I have certainly crossed them. I have utterly, consciously, and with planning aforethought blown it all.
>
> "'I guess I was never a Christian in the first place, because if I had been, I would have made some progress in the Christian life... I'll try going to church for a while longer, but I think I've tried every possible thing the church has told me to do. After that, I guess I'll return to paganism and 'eat, drink, and be merry' for the time I've got left. What else is there to do?'"[34]

Talk about fruits almost always alienates people, because it is always experienced as accusation, even after you believe. If a pastor says, "The Gospel makes us *this* way," an honest young person in the congregation may think, "Then why am I *that* way, instead?" The Gospel does not solve all our problems—in some cases, seemingly none of them. When it does, it is not usually observable or measurable. Mary Karr, a poet, once said that after years of being a Christian, she realized one day she only wants to kill *some* of the people on the New York subway in the morning, whereas she used to want to kill them *all*. When there are fruits,

34. Rod Rosenbladt, *Christ Alone* (Crossway Books, 1999).

this is a good way of talking about them. It is not up, up, up—like threading through a career track or learning how to knit. The Christian life is not like acquiring a skill.

The fruit of grace is also not a result of our efforts, which is, in the optimistic 21st-century West, one of Christianity's most counter-cultural ideas.[35] If we are transformed, it is purely a doing of God. As Fr. Stephen Freeman, an Eastern Orthodox priest and author, wrote:

> "It is, of course, possible to describe the changes that occur in the state of repentance as 'progress,' but this distorts the work that is taking place. In the words of the Elder Sophrony, 'The way down is the way up.' The self-emptying of repentance is not the work of gradual improvement, a work of 'getting better and better.' It is a work of becoming 'lesser and lesser.' We are not saved by moral progress, transformed by our efforts. It is not self-improvement."[36]

The Gospel is for sinners and *remains for sinners*, as long as we're on the earth. The idea that salvation and moral progress thereafter are up to us is called 'Pelagianism,' and the Church condemned it long ago.[37] The idea that salvation is partly up to us, and God does the sanctifying work, is called 'Semipelagianism,' and it was

---

35. The "third use of the Law," which occupies a tiny spot in John Calvin's work and is nonexistent in Luther's, means that the Law is needed as a motivational tool—like a whip to a "lazy sluggish donkey" (Calvin)—to spur the believer to good works. It's needed as a guide. This "third use" has exercised enormous influence in Christianity over the years. In Protestantism, it has grown from a page and a half in Calvin's 1100-page work to the primary theme in many church pulpits. It is assumed that the Gospel of forgiveness is either for non-Christians in the congregation or for relatively new believers, but after a while, our main focus should be on living a better life. This is probably not the dominant theme in Christian history, and it is certainly not one in the work of the Reformers. But because the human heart is always inclined to the Law, to wanting rules and conditions so that we may exercise control, the theme crops up regularly.
36. http://blogs.ancientfaith.com/glory2godforallthings/2015/01/11/st-mary-egypt-moral-progress-2/
37. See St. Augustine, "On Grace and Free Choice," for a magisterial refutation.

also condemned. The idea that God saves us and then the work of moral progress is up to us doesn't really have a name, but it could be classified as a misguided Semipelagianism. It is all up to God.

Take the life of St. Julian the Hospitaller, for example. In the telling of Gustav Flaubert, he was raised in royalty and was told he was destined to kill his parents. He righteously went into exile to avoid this horrible sin. He married and lived comfortably for many years, until one day his old parents sought him out. He was hunting all day, so his wife greeted his parents and allowed them to sleep in her own bedroom. When Julian returned, he saw two people in his marriage bed and went into a jealous rage, killing them both. When he realized what he'd done he went into another self-imposed exile, shackled with self-hatred, and renounced the world. He lived out his days in solitude, ferrying people across a river. When he was old, a disgusting vagabond came into his shack, covered in skin-lesions, asking for shelter. He then asked for warmth, and as Julian embraced him he was revealed to be Christ disguised, and Christ forgave him, and they ascended together into heaven.

The Russian master Leo Tolstoy takes on sanctification in "Father Sergius," a story about a brilliant and virtuous man living in isolation as a monk to mortify his sinful desires. When a beautiful, naked woman tries to seduce him, he righteously cuts off his hand (Mt 5:30) rather than sin, and she flees. Then, after seventeen years of immaculately virtuous living, the proud Sergius can no longer resist, and he has sex with a mentally impaired, underage girl. He flees into exile and lives a life of deep remorse and quiet service to others. Then he is arrested on the road for not having a passport and is deported to Siberia. In a monastic setting with every advantage, Sergius can do nothing in seventeen years because his pride remains intact, perhaps even fuelled by his piety. Once his image of himself is destroyed, however, forgiveness becomes actual to him, and he is freed to serve others. The first fruit of the Gospel is humility.

Firstfruits: Humility

These two stories of sanctification bear almost no resemblance to some churches' fixation on habit-formation, linear progress, moral effort, spiritual empowerment, and feeling 'close to God.' Thus the first fruit of grace is humility: not a lessening of sin so much as a *deeper awareness of sin's continuing presence*. Genuine development of virtue, when it does exist, must feel like a lessening. Sins like lust and greed and stinginess are not fixed by habit-forming and effort, which either lead the repressed tendencies to re-manifest, stronger, at a later point, or to reinforce our obsession with being 'masters of our fate,' which the Bible calls 'pride.' Pride underlies our other sins; they are symptoms of being hung up on ourselves. Taking the Law as motivation and a guide to righteous living—the so-called 'third use'—often feeds our addiction to self. Instead, the Law must continue to convict us of our utter unrighteousness, and the Gospel must continue to save us. Again, the first fruit of the Gospel is *humility*, which means something between self-awareness (as a sinner!) and self-forgetfulness. Jean-Luc Marion, a Catholic philosopher, sums it up perfectly:[38]

> "Through a performative contradiction that is intuitively irrefutable, someone who lays claim to sanctity disproves it in him- or her-self. Why can't holiness lay claim to itself? Not only because one does not want to fall into massive trap of pride in one's own satisfaction and self-affirmation, which is involved, but above all because holiness is unaware of itself…The false prophet, like the false saint, always stands out conspicuously by the fact that this affirmation [of holiness] may never be questioned."

As a final note, in our self-help culture 'repentance' is usually taken to mean an outward change in action. That may be a

---

38. "The Invisibility of the Saint," in *Faith Without Borders* (Chicago UP, 2011).

part of it, over the long run, but the Greek, *metanoia*, means 'after-thought.' Repentance primarily means contrition, the thought and emotion that should pop into one's head after doing something wrong. It is to turn away from one's sin—and sinful self!—in the spontaneous way we might turn away from a perfect ribeye steak if we saw a worm in it. Unless this moment comes first, a change in action can work the opposite of repentance. The Old Adam, who must be righteous and will never accept blame (Gen 3:12), is alive and well in believers. The idea that we will be better people next week, next month, when we get a new job, or when we finally move to Austin, Texas is far more fun to think (and talk!) about than our ongoing sin. This orientation toward the future can be a distraction from the reality that we are still sinners.

When confronted with our own failure, many of us see it as an opportunity to redouble our trust in willpower and optimism. '*I've been* struggling with this (you rarely hear the present-tense), but...' 'Things are hard, but good.' To throw oneself upon grace instead requires radical humility and will often feel like death—like one's virtue or willpower are being stripped away. This is merely the long and ongoing, never-complete process of recognizing who we really are, which Christ's freedom from condemnation gives us the freedom to do. "What's the difference between a Christian and a non-Christian?" a college mentor used to quip. "...A Christian is someone who knows she's no different from anyone else." That's what humility means, and it usually feels like humiliation.

Receptivity

The feature of being more receptive, or open, to new people and experiences is another possible fruit of hearing the Gospel and taking it to heart. The person who knows herself to be a sinner, saved by an act of grace from beyond herself, will know that something as broken as a human being cannot fix itself. She will therefore be likely to learn from others and look to solutions from others, because she is constantly fumbling for truth, beauty, and goodness, which she knows herself to possess in a *very* limited quantity.

She may, for instance, not feel the need to avoid a 'secular' movie, even a depraved one, because she knows she has something to learn from it. She may not exhibit rarefied taste in books, movies or music—she's just looking for anything that helps. Subjected to a horrible sermon, she might be more likely to be grateful for the helpful 5% than critical of the misinformed 95%—indeed, she may not consciously make the distinction. (She certainly will not write a whole tract on Law and Gospel!) Nadia Bolz-Weber, a Lutheran pastor, was once fuming to her husband against the wrong kind of Christians, and he told her that "every time we draw a line between us and others, Jesus is always on the other side of it."[39]

The receptive person will, therefore, not be interested in *criticism* but in *help*. She will be more interested in others' opinions than her own. Most Christian authors, including the ones of this book, are a little weak when it comes to receptivity. Sometimes pastors are weak on it, too. The person who's best at it, out of all your friends, is probably the one who comes off as overemotional and a little insane—someone deeply, deeply interested in *help*. Or they are eight years old (Mt 18:3), because if you know that everything true, good, and beautiful comes as a gift, how can you not be receptive? It follows pretty naturally from humility, but is easily sabotaged by high levels of competence, knowledge, or taste. Perhaps receptivity is the reason why laypersons, more so than theologians, are often the ones who have visions of things like the Virgin Mary—because their eyes are open for *help*.

---

39. Nadia Bolz-Weber, *Pastrix* (Jericho Books, 2013).

The person who knows herself to be a sinner is also less likely to buy into the permanence of her own plans. In this regard, receptivity entails passivity. Because she doesn't have the highest view of her own personal capabilities, she can understand God (and the world at large) as operating more or less beyond her sphere of control. She is resigned to relinquish what control she believed she had in deference to a God who had it all along. She may prefer slowing down and waiting over acting and getting, listening over speaking, the admission of her own uncertainty over the firm insistence she used to depend on. She no longer needs that insistence for the truth to remain true; she has been delivered from the world of self-reliance and control. This fruit of the gospel, then, is cruciform in nature—it is the death of one's own sense of propriety. Robert Farrar Capon describes it as the difference between a dead hand and a living one:

> "I want you to hold out your right hand, palm up, and imagine that someone is placing, one after another, all sorts of good gifts in it. Make the good things whatever you like—M & Ms, weekends in Acapulco, winning the lottery, falling in love, having perfect children, being wise, talented, good-looking, and humble besides—anything. But now consider. There are two ways your hand can respond to those goods. It can respond to them as a live hand and try to clutch, to hold onto the single good that is in it at any given moment—thus closing itself to all other possible goods; or it can respond as a dead hand—in which case it will simply lie there perpetually open to all the goods in the comings and the goings of their dance... Jesus, obviously, was not without an interest in life: his reputation as a glutton and winebibber was not gained by sitting at home eating tofu and drinking herb tea. But equally obviously, Jesus did not count his life—either divine or human—a thing to be grasped at."[40]

---

40. *Kingdom, Grace, Judgment* (Eerdmans, 2002).

So where the Law is a closed fist, the Gospel is an open hand. Where the Law is the life of continued control and self-preservation, the Gospel is the open readiness for resonances of truth and comfort, anywhere and everywhere.

Gratitude

Imagine you fall off the side of an ocean liner and, not knowing how to swim, begin to drown. Someone on the deck spots you, flailing in the water and throws you a life preserver. It lands directly in front of you and, just before losing consciousness, you grab hold for dear life. They pull you up onto the deck, and you cough the water out of your lungs. People gather around, rejoicing that you are safe and waiting expectantly while you regain your senses. After you finally catch your breath, you open your mouth and say: "Did you see the way I grabbed onto that life preserver?! How tightly I held on to it?! Did you notice the definition in my biceps and the dexterity of my wrists? I was all over that thing!"[41]

Needless to say, it would be a bewildering and borderline insane response.[42] To draw attention to the way *you* cooperated with the rescue effort denigrates the whole point of what happened, which is that you were saved. A much more likely chain of events is that you would immediately seek out the person who threw the life preserver, and you would thank them. Not just superficially, either. You would embrace them, ask them their name, invite them to dinner, maybe give them your cabin!

Gratitude is a natural response to salvation. It does not require coercion or encouragement; to the extent that the individual understands what has happened, gratitude will flow organically and abundantly from their heart. The precise form it takes will be

---

41. This example comes from John Z's *Grace in Addiction* (Mockingbird, 2012), which adapts it from a talk by Rod Rosenbladt.
42. And depressingly, a common one.

different every time, but such is the nature of fruit.

In fact, what's interesting about gratitude is its immunity to exertion. For example, we all remember our parents telling us when we were young to say thank you to our grandparents or teachers or friends. We may have said the words, but good manners were seldom, if ever, able to produce the feeling of gratitude itself. The same applies to preachers who instruct their congregations to give thanks (and in such-and-such a fashion). If the feeling isn't there, no amount of pleading will engender it. It will likely backfire (Rm 5:20).

Gratitude also happens to be the closest approximation, emotionally, of happiness. In 2011, *The New York Times* reported that feelings of gratitude have "been linked to better health, sounder sleep, less anxiety and depression, higher long-term satisfaction with life and kinder behavior toward others, including romantic partners."[43] The fruit bears fruit of its own, it would appear. No wonder the *Times* calls Thanksgiving "the most psychologically correct holiday."

The Protestant Reformers, it turns out, beat the social scientists to the punch by nearly five hundred years when they underlined the importance of Law-Gospel preaching. Martin Luther himself saw the pulpit as the platform from which people hear, week after week, about the goodness of God's grace in light of human failure and sin. In other words, church is the place where we get in touch with divine generosity, and therefore gratitude, on a weekly basis. Where the resentments and entitlements that build up throughout the week are squashed under the weight of the Law, and hope and faith are born afresh (and unbidden) as we unwrap the Gift anew. Which is not only what God wants for us, but also the best thing for us. Teaching, encouragement, guidance, wisdom, challenge (gulp!)—as important as those things may be, they are no match for gratitude when it comes to

---

43. John Tierney, "A Serving of Gratitude May Save the Day," Nov. 21, 2011.

reviving the spirits and inspiring works of love. Thank God for that.

Love

While Law has the tendency to incite resentment, the Gospel has the remarkable tendency to inspire acts of love. This is because the Gospel, the message of God's unrestrained and irrevocable Yes to humankind, is a message of love without condition. It is a form of love we do not know very well, but if we've ever glimpsed it, we know it is life-changing. Belovedness can actually beget love itself. As the Bible says: "We love because he first loved us" (1 Jn 4:19).

Most of the love we experience—from parents, from friends, from husbands and wives—is a narrow shadow of this love. Even in these intimate relationships we have the propensity to love with ulterior motive, with standards and stipulations.

In a world that values honesty and vulnerability about as much as it values the stomach flu, this is not the way to 'love.' You love someone like this, we say, and they will walk all over you. You give them ice cream, and they will do what you say, but only because you are paying them. The only real way to get respect is to hold a loved one accountable, and not give them an inch of wiggle room until they've paid up. To give without expectation of receiving is a quick road to bankruptcy, they'll tell you. Maybe they are right. Relational bankruptcy, though, may be the only way to get into the business of unconditional love.

Unconditional love has a completely different *modus operandi*: Go for broke. Let it go. Spill it. God's love is typified by foolish perseverance. It stands in direct contradiction to the common sense of a prudish business model. God's love doesn't invest a little love in the hope that you grow it into something bigger—if that were the case, you would be conditionally covered, and conditionally dropped. It risks the farm, leaves everything on the table. In fact, unconditional love doesn't think about how much it is investing—anything less than everything is too little—or about how much it might get in return. That's irrelevant to why it went into the business in the first place. Love gives everything because it gives everything. It dies to itself out of a desire to see the other live. Unconditional love cannot be snuffed out because it has already snuffed itself out on your behalf. And it has a strange way of re-igniting in the most illustrious ways.

We see it in the radical resurrection of characters like Jean Valjean in *Les Miserables*. And sometimes, if we're lucky, we hear of it happening in real life. *The New York Times*'s "Modern Love" column once told the story of a wife foolishly standing beside a husband who, for months, told her he no longer wanted to be with her and the kids:

> "And, yeah, you can bet I wanted to sit him down and persuade him to stay. To love me. To fight for what we've created. You can bet I wanted to. But I didn't. I barbecued. Made lemonade. Set the table for four. Loved him from afar.
>
> And one day, there he was, home from work early, mowing the lawn. A man doesn't mow his lawn if he's going to leave it. Not this man. Then he fixed a door that had been broken for eight years. He made a comment about our front porch needing paint. Our front porch. He mentioned needing wood for next winter. The future. Little by little, he started talking about the future.
>
> It was Thanksgiving dinner that sealed it. My husband bowed his head humbly and said, 'I'm thankful for my family.'"

This is belovedness softening the heart. This is love producing what judgment can't.

Spontaneity

The Gospel of God's grace also provokes spontaneity, an inherent trust that the grace which moved someone like you is bound to move pretty much anywhere. Like those disciples who were called by Jesus and immediately left their fishing nets and cash boxes and family obligations, spontaneity is the sudden and oftentimes foolish 'yes' to the call of God.

In life, there is a phenomenon known as the Nazareth Principle. It comes from the story a man named Nathanael who is invited to meet Jesus and, upon finding out that this God-man hails from a backwater, scoffs, "Can anything good come out of Nazareth?" (Jn 1:46). Nathanael's lovable, gut-level response is totally natural. The Nazareth Principle applies to us all; our basic human tendency is to distrust anything that does not appeal to the 'glory-story' we have in mind. We have an intrinsic confirmation bias that no-name losers do not make good friends, that losing teams do not win championships, that 'simple' people have nothing to teach us. On the contrary, Jesus is proof—in his life, death, and resurrection—that *everything* good can come out of Nazareth. Spontaneity is the spirit of this trust.

Spontaneity is the opposite of fear. As opposed to fear, which closes off peripheral options and 'sticks with the plan,' spontaneity remains foolishly open to possibility. It may appear to the world like childish naïveté or whimsy, but really it is a fuller trust in the nature of the gift.

Jesus talks about spontaneity as being "born of the spirit": "the spirit blows where it chooses, and you hear the sound of it, but you do not know where it comes from, or where it goes" (Jn 3:8). In this way, the nature of Holy Spirit is akin to the nature of imagination and improvisation. It creates rules of its own and does not lead in any specific direction. The Holy Spirit, which Jesus says cannot be conjured or manipulated, creates a way out of no way, a somebody out of a nobody. The Holy Spirit ignites possibility in places where no one would expect to find it, and spontaneity remains to open to its direction.

Spontaneity is also, therefore, utterly playful. Child's play and leisure completely disregard the world of costs and benefits, of means and ends. Instead, someone at play is completely immersed the infinite riches of the present moment. A child could not tell you this is what they are doing, precisely because they're not thinking of it—they are simply allowed to create something out of nothing.

So while the Law calculates, the Gospel improvises. While the Law seeks the most effective and efficient route, the Gospel provides the willingness to take the back roads and get lost. While the Law looks over a shoulder for a better conversation to be having, the Gospel inspires the conversation at hand, entrusting full well that you are exactly where you need to be.

Humor

Speaking of childlikeness, it is apt that these fruits of the Gospel would come back around to their firstfruit, humility, in a different expression—*humor*. If the Gospel is ever experienced for the ridiculous good news that it is, then laughter is soon to follow it. And this is mostly because humor is, in part, an expression of relief. Steve Brown describes it perfectly in his story about a woman who, after years of hiding a moment of infidelity from her husband, suddenly feels the (spontaneous!) need to admit it to him. Though nervous, she decides to do it.

> "I saw her the next day, and she looked fifteen years younger. 'What happened?' I asked. 'When I told him,' she exclaimed, 'he replied that he had known about the incident for twenty years and was just waiting for me to tell him so he could tell me how much he loved me!' And then she started to laugh. 'He forgave me twenty years ago, and I've been needlessly carrying all this guilt for all these years!' Perhaps you are like this woman who had been forgiven and didn't know it."[44]

Her laughter is the laughter of the forgiven. It stems from a simultaneous flood of relief ("He forgave me twenty years ago!")

---

44. "The Laughter of God," *When Being Good Isn't Good Enough* (Keylife, 2014).

and a corresponding lack of self-seriousness ("How ridiculous that I carried this around for so long?"). A sense of humor comes from the ridiculousness of your happy outcome, and the fact that it had nothing to do with you.

Humor and hyperbole are, then, delicate ministers of God's good relief. In various ways, either through satire or self-deprecation, humor is a way of uncoupling the truth from its sting. It is a way of including oneself on the wrong side of the righteousness equation. It is a delightful willingness to be wrong, because you can afford to be. It also allows us the privilege of disarming the stings against us, to find humor in things around us that might have offended or wounded us before.

Humor can also be used as a form of gracious misdirection. It is a chance for the forgiven to put on a clown suit in love, for the sake of deflecting another's judgment. This is precisely what Christ does for the woman caught in adultery, lining out a distracting drawing in the sand for her team of accusers (Jn 8:6). If we are so lucky, we experience the same willingness to play the fool, to feel the great pricelessness of God's wonderful gift, and thus to ham it up at no cost to anyone.

In the realm of the Law, we must keep face. In the realm of the Gospel, we can laugh at our own faces in the mirror. In the realm of the Law, we must tediously craft emails with the right balance of seriousness and brevity. In the realm of the Gospel, we're free to say precisely the ridiculous thing that comes to mind, without fear of what brand of trouble our words may bring. While the Law incites us to point our fingers at others in blame, the Gospel provokes us to return the pointing finger back to our chest, and shrug our shoulders, and laugh at the absurdity.[45]

---

45. Surely humor is part of what is meant by the meaning of pure love "casting out fear" (1 Jn 4:18). When we are out of the realm of fear, we are into the realm where self-ridicule is easy.

Freedom

All of these fruits stem from a message of freedom that turns everything on its head. On the surface, this freedom may change everything, or change nothing at all. It may push one to willingly and liberally surrender all their 'five-year plans' and take a cross-country road trip—and push another to keep everything as-is. Who knows, the fact that we are valued unconditionally might even loosen the knot, just a bit, of all those little-l laws which snare us at every turn. Not that it *has* to—the fruit of the Gospel is more and more freedom, the unfettered and unconditional acceptance of a sinner, whether he or she does anything about it at all.

'It's easier said than done,' absolutely, but that is precisely the point. None of these fruits of the Gospel are Action Items to be laid out and performed. They do not come with a Compendium of Fruit Growth so you can compare with rigorous attention to your progress. It would be nice if we felt the presence of these fruits in our lives once a year! Once a lifetime! But the question becomes, then, why would Christ have "set us free" if it's not about getting more, getting better fruit?

Luckily, we are given the answer in Scripture, albeit not a very satisfying one: He freed us *for freedom*. Not for a return on his investment, not for world domination, not even for more credit. In complete repudiation of output and reform, Christ's offering is one-way: "It is for freedom that Christ has set us free" (Gal 5:1).

OBJECTIVE COMFORT

In conclusion, the life of the believer may get better, but it often feels like it is getting worse—becoming more aware of one's weaknesses, more remorseful of one's failures, more foolish or absurd or even contemptible to the eyes of others, like David shedding his dignity and dancing "as any vulgar fellow might" (2 Sam 6:20). The snares of conscience, however, and the voices of doubt continue. After the first seventeen-year phase of what was to become an extraordinary lifetime of showing God's love, Mother Teresa penned the following lines in her journal:

> "You have thrown away as unwanted — unloved. I call, I cling, I want — and there is no One to answer — no One on Whom I can cling — no, No One. — Alone... Where is my Faith — even deep down right in there is nothing, but emptiness & darkness — My God — how painful is this unknown pain — I have no Faith — I dare not utter the words & thoughts that crowd in my heart — & make me suffer untold agony."

She was lucky to later enjoy a reprieve of several weeks, after which her feelings of desolation returned and stayed with her for decades, one of the most exemplary lights of God's love undergoing excruciating emptiness and doubt. As much as we inveterate optimists yearn for empowerment, assurance, and control, what fruits of the Spirit there are will often look like desolation. Luther used the term *simul iustus et peccator*—justified and sinner at once—and we live in both these identities. We experience mainly just the sinner, but the justification is hidden in Christ, and thus all the more real.

The Gospel is therefore *objective comfort*: We cannot let our own moral failings or spiritual desolation be the measure of God's mercy, because the measure of God's mercy is Christ. We do not look hard for the effects of God's mercy upon the stubborn human heart, no more than a child, given a toy at Christmas, thinks, "How much am I enjoying this? Is it making me love my parents any more? Is it making me a better son or daughter? Since my parents love me, am I mirroring that love to others?" No, the child simply plays, and enjoys. The gift is in no way contingent upon the response.

The measure of God's mercy is Christ. The signs of transformation as a result of the Gospel are mostly illegible, and the true saint would have little desire to read them if they were. The measure of the believer's state of virtue or holiness, therefore, is also Christ. We so often approach our faith as if it were a call to traverse the distance between man and God, ensconced even in our language of growing 'closer' to God. "To open up again the abyss closed in Jesus Christ," Karl Barth wrote, "cannot be our task."[46] There is not distance, only the God who is, in Meister Eckhart's words, "nearer to me than I am to myself." To look for assurance from the effects, of fruits, is to re-open the distance between man and God, undermining the very thing it seeks. God's presence and promise are objective comfort, not to be conjured or obtained but only *recognized*. Thus while we change continually for better and worse, God is unchanging. Barth continues:

---

46. *The Humanity of God* (Westminster John Knox, 1996).

A Theology for Sinners (and Saints)

> "The man with whom we have to do in ourselves and in others, though a rebel, a sluggard, a hypocrite, is likewise the creature to whom his Creator is faithful and not unfaithful. But there is still more: he is the being whom God has loved, loves, and will love, because He has substituted Himself in Jesus Christ and made Himself the guarantee."

We are called to simply believe a truth which has been accomplished by God *for us*, one mercifully immune to our feelings, vacillations, and continued doubts and shortcomings. Those old selves "have died," and their lives are "hidden with Christ in God" (Col 3:3). What we feel and perceive is the death of those old selves, but their resurrection and new lives are hidden. Thus the wild, absurd, unconditional truth of God's love in Emmanuel—"God with us," just as we are "with Christ"—is one we may not always feel, but something to simply be repeated to us over and over until some shred of it sinks in. Though hidden, these new lives are secure with Christ our savior "in God," who is always the same: "If we are faithless, he remains faithful—for he cannot deny himself" (2 Tim 2:13). The Gospel thus remains true as God is true. "It is finished," and there is nothing more to be done.

APPENDIX: DISTINGUISHING
BETWEEN LAW AND GOSPEL

"The distinction between law and gospel is the highest
art in Christendom"
–Martin Luther[47]

A strong belief of Luther, and those who follow in his footsteps,
is that people should not be enticed to church by the Gospel
and then, after believing, turn toward self-improvement. The
Law always kills, and the Spirit always gives life. This death and
resurrection of the believer is not a one-time event, but must
be repeated continually: It is the shape of the Christian life. On
Sundays, therefore, some form of the Law is ideally preached
to kill, and the Gospel to vivify—"the letter kills, but the Spirit
gives life" (2 Cor 3:6).[48] But in many situations, the Law is mistakenly preached to give life, on the assumption that the believer,
unlike the new Christian, has the moral strength to follow the
guidelines. This leads to burnout, often producing agnostics or

---

47. *Weimarer Ausgabe*, 36:41.31.

48. It depends on the congregation, of course. Lord knows there are plenty of
burned-out Christians who are already 'dead' in self-recrimination, and perhaps
there are even a few in places who could stand to have their conscience height-
ened. We tend to err on the side of assuming the former.

converts to Eastern Orthodoxy. Words like 'accountability' or 'intentionality,' for example, are sure signs that the letter, rather than the Spirit, is being looked to for life. To help distinguish this form of misguided Law from the Gospel, here's a handy guide:

1. Listen for a distortion of the commandment: Anytime a hard commandment is softened, such as "Be perfect" (Mt 5:48) to "just do your best," we're looking to the Law, not the Gospel, for life.

2. Discern the balance of agency: If you're in charge of making it happen, it's misguided Law. If God's in charge, it's Gospel. If it's a mixture, it's Law.

3. Look for honesty: If you or others either seem 'A-okay' or 'struggling, but...,' then likely it's because the Old Adam is alive and well (there will also be a horrible scandal in the next three months). If people are open and honest about their problems, such freedom shows the Gospel is at work.

4. Watch for exhaustion: If the yoke is hard and the burden heavy week after week, then the letter's probably overpowering the Spirit.

5. Examine the language: If you hear 'If... then,' 'Wouldn't it be nice...,' 'We should all...,' or anything else that smacks of the imperative voice, it's implicit works-salvation. If you hear the indicative voice—'God is...,' 'We are...,' or 'God will...'—then it's probably Gospel.

6. Watch for the view of human nature, or anthropology: If human willpower, strength, or effort are being lauded or appealed to, it's Law. High anthropology means low Christology, and vice-versa.

7. Finally, keep an eye out for the 'Galatians effect,' summarized by St. Paul:

> "Did you receive the Spirit by doing the works of the

law or by believing what you heard? Are you so foolish? Having started with the Spirit, are you now ending with the flesh? Did you experience so much for nothing?—if it really was for nothing. Well then, does God supply you with the Spirit and work miracles among you by your doing the works of the law, or by your believing what you heard?" (Gal 3:2-5)

If how you're approaching or being told to approach Christianity now feels different from "believing what you heard," we're in Galatians territory. Christianity is Good News, and it never ceases to be Good News.

APPENDIX: WHAT ABOUT ANTINOMIANISM?

There's an accusation sometimes leveled against those who stress Christian freedom and forgiveness in lieu of behavior-modification, and who downplay 'spiritual progress' as a burdensome distraction from the indiscriminate compassion of grace. The charge is that such people denigrate God's law, or cast it as 'bad.' The formal name for this charge is 'antinomianism' (*anti*=against, *nomos*=law). The common picture of the antinomian is someone who thinks that, because of Christ's forgiveness, they can (and will) do whatever they want: self-indulgence, sexual deviancy, substance abuse, lewd music, and the like. A few points to make:

1. If you're not being accused of antinomianism occasionally, you're probably not preaching the Gospel. St. Paul himself had to answer criticism on precisely this point.

2. Paul evidently thought a lot about the antinomian gripe, and responded in no uncertain terms: "Should we continue in sin that grace may abound?," he imagines a satire of his message going. "By no means!" he replies. "How can we who have died to sin go on living in it?" (Rm 6:1-2). To the extent that we have

Law and Gospel

died to sin, it's simply impossible to go on living in it. Of course, none of us have died to sin entirely, or even mostly.

3. Which is why antinomians (in the hedonistic sense) don't really exist. The specter of a depraved hedonist sustained by a fervent belief in the Gospel is just that, a specter—there aren't real people who live that way. There may be real people who use forgiveness as an excuse to keep on doing bad stuff—but if there are, it's not as though the gospel of behavior-modification would've gotten them in the church's door instead. In fact, their self-indulgence itself is often a response to the law rather than a (fictional) disregard of it, rebellion and conformity being flip sides of the same coin (see also: Fight, Flight and Appeasement). As John D. Koch and Simeon Zahl wrote:

> "Martin Luther once made a remarkable comment about antinomianism. He called it a drama put on in an empty theater. What he meant essentially was that antinomianism doesn't really exist. That is, sure you can say you are an antinomian, and you can have behavior to match, but no one can ever really be free of the Law like that. It is built into the world, built into our lives. No one can outrun every 'ought,' however much they might like to, not even the most libertine of us all. This is why antinomianism has been called an 'impossible heresy.'"[49]

4. The true antinomian is the one who tries to distort the Law. The one who reads "Be perfect, therefore, as your heavenly Father is perfect" (Mt 5:48) as "Do your best, that's all anyone can ask." Or who read "Sell what you own, and give the money to the poor" as "Tithe ten percent" or "Contribute what you reasonably can." The very people who accuse others of antinomianism are usually the ones who are themselves denigrating the Law. Because if you want measurable spiritual progress or spiritual accomplishment, you're going to have lower God's standard quite a bit.

---

49. From http://www.mbird.com/glossary/antinomian/

5. The antidote to antinomianism, therefore, is not to sell people on linear, measurable sanctification, but to preach the Law in all its fullness. The condemning voice of conscience should not be smoothed over by developing good habits, but should be echoed in the pulpit and taken to its extreme, as Christ does in Matthew 5. *The only genuine way to relate to the Law is to be utterly condemned by it.* Anything less—including using it for exhortation—risks real antinomianism.

APPENDIX: THE 'HORIZONTAL' AND THE 'VERTICAL'

As noted in the main text, the little-l laws of society function almost identically to the Big-L Law of God on the person who hears them, especially those little-l laws which are most personal, the ones around which we've shaped our identity, such as Thou Shalt Be successful, wealthy, skinny, busy, wise, and so forth. They may be 'horizontal' in nature—they govern how we relate to those on our own 'plane,' namely, i.e., ourselves and other human beings—but they often have the same impact as the vertical ones, which concern the relationship of those who are below (us) to that which is above (God).

A similar corollary exists between the 'Big-G' Gospel of Jesus Christ and 'little-g' grace in human affairs, or love in the midst of deserved judgment. While we sometimes use the terms Gospel and grace interchangeably, the 'G's are dicier territory than the 'L's. A few things to note on this analogy between 'vertical' Law/Gospel and 'horizontal' law/grace:

1. Just as the Law of God fails to produce righteousness, expectations in society tend to fail to produce what they demand. Likewise, just as the Gospel of God *may* produce righteousness

in believers, positive change in human affairs can often be traced back to some experience of one-way love. Well-adjusted people tend to be those whose parents expressed unconditional love more than demanding certain behaviors.

2. Because God's Gospel is one of grace, we can sometimes better understand it by looking at examples of grace from the 'horizontal' level. This is one reason the Bible calls God a Father and us children; in ideal parent-child relationships, one-way love without conditions or strings attached, and a nearly boundless capacity for forgiving the child, are the order of the day.

3. The sort of love without conditions which creates change on the horizontal level, however, cannot be engineered. "The Spirit blows where it will," after all. So attempts to demonstrate grace, if they are not heartfelt and spontaneous, risk degenerating into silent expectations, passive-aggression, and small resentments—in other words, a new law. Which means that the fact that acts of grace tend to produce healthy change in their targets cannot be reduced to a technique or a strategy for influencing/manipulating other people. They'll usually see through it to the confusing morass of unsaid expectation underneath. Repressing a conflict is not the same as defusing it.

4. Distinctions between the horizontal and the vertical are important if we are to avoid conflating the way we think about God and the way we think about human life. If you're feeling guilty for being stingy, for example, recognizing and asking for forgiveness is probably the best way to handle it. But if you're feeling insecure about a receding hairline, it may be best to recognize the problem and then remember that as far as God is concerned, it doesn't really matter.

5. Finally, in preaching, examples of human expectations fostering rebellion and human grace breathing life are crucial for connecting one's hearer to the material emotionally and making

the categories come alive. But illustrations are only illustrations. Meaning, they are meant to point to the underlying predicament rather than distract from it: The problem itself is the Law, the solution the Gospel—not their horizontal echoes.

FOR FURTHER READING

On Being a Theologian of the Cross: Reflections on Luther's Heidelberg Disputation, by Gerhard Forde

Grace in Practice: A Theology of Everyday Life, by Paul F. M. Zahl

Kingdom, Grace, Judgment: Paradox, Outrage, and Vindication in the Parables of Jesus, by Robert Farrar Capon

Law and Gospel: How to Read and Apply the Bible, by C. F. W. Walther

Martin Luther's Theology: A Contemporary Interpretation, by Oswald Bayer

The Merciful Impasse: The Sermon on the Mount for People Who've Crashed (and Burned), by Paul F. M. Zahl (DVD)

Mistakes Were Made (but not by me), by Carol Tavris and Elliot Aronson

The Mockingbird Devotional: Good News for Today (and Every Day), edited by Ethan Richardson and Sean Norris

ALSO FROM MOCKINGBIRD

The Mockingbird: A quarterly magazine

A Mess of Help: From the Crucified Soul of Rock N' Roll, by David Zahl

Eden and Afterward: A Mockingbird Guide to Genesis, by William McDavid

PZ's Panopticon: An Off-the-Wall Guide to World Religion, by Paul F. M. Zahl

The Mockingbird Devotional: Good News for Today (and Every Day), edited by Ethan Richardson and Sean Norris

Grace in Addiction: The Good News of Alcoholics Anonymous for Everybody, by John Z

The Merciful Impasse: The Sermon on the Mount for Those Who've Crashed (and Burned), by Paul F. M. Zahl

This American Gospel: Public Radio Parables and the Grace of God, by Ethan Richardson

Our books are available at www.mbird.com/publications or on Amazon, and our magazine can be found at magazine.mbird.com.

ABOUT MOCKINGBIRD

Founded in 2007, Mockingbird is an organization devoted to connecting the Christian faith with the realities of everyday life in fresh and down-to-earth ways. We do this primarily, but not exclusively, through our publications, conferences, and online resources. To find out more, visit us at mbird.com or e-mail us at info@mbird.com.

CPSIA information can be obtained at www.ICGtesting.com
Printed in the USA
LVOW04s0530150615

442484LV00031B/960/P